FROM "THE
CONTAINED
NEW
MISSION SUCCESS!

*I will live this day as if it were Christmas. I will be
a giver of gifts and deliver to my enemies the gift of
forgiveness; my opponents, tolerance; my friends, a
smile; my children, a good example, and every gift
will be wrapped with unconditional love.*

Og Mandino

MISSION: SUCCESS!

BANTAM BOOKS

TORONTO • NEW YORK • LONDON • SYDNEY • AUCKLAND

MISSION: SUCCESS!

A Bantam Book
Bantam hardcover edition / July 1986
Bantam paperback edition / June 1987

Library of Congress Cataloging-in-Publication Data

Mandino, Og.
  Mission: success!

  1. Success.   I. Title.
  BJ1611.2.M3236   1986   158'.1   84-48268
  ISBN 0-553-26500-8

Published simultaneously in the United States and Canada

Bantam Books are published by Bantam Books, a division of Bantam
Doubleday Dell Publishing Group, Inc. Its trademark, consisting of the
words "Bantam Books" and the portrayal of a rooster, is Registered in
U.S. Patent and Trademark Office and in other countries. Marca
Registrada. Bantam Books, 666 Fifth Avenue, New York, New York
10103.

PRINTED IN THE UNITED STATES OF AMERICA

KR   0 9 8 7 6 5 4 3

Dedicated, with love,
to a very special man,
PAUL PLAYTON

More than once you have heard me say that life is a mission most of us are trying to fly without any flight plan because they never gave us one in school. Life is indeed a mission . . . but we must remember that every day is a life in miniature. . . .

—Winnie Marlow

Therefore, since we are being observed by so great a cloud of witnesses who have gone before us, let us rid ourselves of all things that hinder us and let us run with courage and endurance the race that is set before us.

Hebrews 12:1

MISSION: SUCCESS!

I

When my half-empty flight on the Concorde touched down at Heathrow Airport, the entire advance contingent of Gardiner Industries, as I expected, was waiting inside the terminal.

"Welcome to London, Mr. Gardiner! After two miserable weeks, even the sun decided to show itself for you today."

"Thank you, Sidney. How's my advertising and publicity genius? Is everything set for a memorable introduction to our British friends tomorrow?"

"Yes, sir," he said, smiling nervously, "I'll review the entire schedule for you on the way to the hotel."

I moved slowly through my eager group of executives, shaking hands, embracing, and answering endless questions on what it had felt like traveling in a graceful white missile faster than the speed of sound. After the usual delays for luggage and customs, Sidney guided me outside toward a black Rolls-Royce. A white-haired uniformed chauffeur stood stiffly at attention, holding the rear door open for us.

"First class, Sidney?"

"Just want to make you feel at home, sir. If you can drive around Scottsdale in a Corniche convertible, there's no reason why you shouldn't have at least a Silver Cloud in London."

As soon as we had settled back in the soft leather, Sidney unzipped his briefcase, removed a legal pad, and began his briefing. Ground-breaking ceremonies for the three-story complex that would house the first foreign branch of Starcrest, Inc., one of the nineteen companies in the Gardiner Industries conglomerate, was scheduled for two o'clock the next afternoon. The building site, in Hampstead Heath, was only about twenty minutes from our hotel. We would all depart from the Dorchester Hotel at one-thirty.

It was difficult to concentrate on what Sidney was saying. I forced myself. A large tent, he droned on, had been erected to shelter the invited dignitaries in case it rained. Following my brief speech, after turning some earth with a gold shovel for the newspaper and television cameras, I would conduct at least a thirty-minute press conference. The vastness of my corporate holdings, and certainly my wealth, he reminded me, would undoubtedly be the prime focus of reporter interest. American capital had virtually ignored Great Britain during the past several decades. Why was Gardiner Industries making such a huge financial commitment?

Names on traffic signs began to divert my attention as we headed toward London. Greenford, Eton, Basingstoke, Hounslow, Ealing . . .

Winnie! I almost spoke her name aloud.

Winnie Marlow, where are you? What happened to you? I closed my eyes and I could still see her pale, lined face with those large green eyes filled with tears as she held me close, kissed my cheeks and repeated, many times, that I was to write often.

December 1944. Forty years. A long time ago. I did write often, for a year or more. A few of my letters came back marked "Gone away" or "No longer at this address." I have no idea what happened to the rest of them, but she never responded. Not even a postcard. How could she have closed the door between us forever, especially after she had dispatched me on a life-long mission? I had fulfilled her mission, far beyond my wildest dreams and possibly hers, but all my victories would have been so much sweeter if she had known.

"Sir, sir?" Sidney's monotone had risen several octaves. "Are you okay?"

"I'm fine," I replied, "just doing a little wool-gathering."

He let his briefcase slide to the floor and crossed his legs. "You were stationed here during the war, weren't you?"

"Yes. Eighth Air Force. Bombardier, in B-24's. Up north or northeast, I guess. Our field was near a village called Marley."

"Did you get to London often?"

"Not often enough. Five or six times during my tour of duty. Flew thirty combat missions."

"And you've never been back to England?"

"No. There was a marriage followed by quite a few jobs while I was trying to find myself, then the kids, then my own first small business, and I just got busier and busier as the years rolled by."

He chuckled. "That's putting it mildly. What a fantastic career you've enjoyed, sir." He pointed at the landscape speeding by. "Does any of this look familiar to you?"

"Not really. We never spent much time sight-seeing when we hit here on those short forty-eight-hour leaves."

"I'll bet you didn't, sir." He smiled, then he shook his head. "You truly have had an amazing life, Mr. Gardiner. From what I know about you, there wasn't much except the clothes on your back and your severance pay when you returned from combat and were separated from the Army Air Force in 1945. And no family. Now here you are returning as one of the wealthiest men in the world. What a story! I hope you'll touch on some of that in your speech tomorrow. Just points out, so dramatically, what a great land of opportunity we live in back in the U.S.A. Are you going to cover that?"

"Yes, but in a slightly different way."

"Oh," he said cautiously, "are you planning to go beyond what we've included in our press release?"

"I haven't seen our press release."

He unzipped his briefcase once more and handed me the three pages of public relations material that had been supplied to the media. I read it and handed it back.

"Well done, Sidney."

"Does that pretty much cover the points you will make, sir?" he persisted.

"Just about." I turned and stared out the window. If

4

he only knew . . . but then, I wasn't sure that Sidney could handle surprises.

The Rolls eased its way through Hammersmith and turned onto Cromwell Road. Soon after we passed the Victoria and Albert Museum we were on Brompton Road, and I leaned forward to get a better look at that magnificent old department store, Harrods.

"We're almost at the hotel, sir."

"I know. I recall that Harrods was not far from Hyde Park."

At last we turned left at Hyde Park Corner on to Park Lane, and the Rolls glided to a stop.

"Welcome to the Dorchester, sir. I'm sure you will enjoy your suite as well as the fantastic service here and you'll find that the food in the Terrace restaurant is unsurpassed."

A smiling bellhop patiently held open my door, but I made no move to exit my comfortable confines. Sidney waited, furrow marks gradually deepening on his pale forehead. I glanced at my watch.

"Sidney, when is my first corporate obligation?"

"Not until three, sir. The BBC is dispatching a television crew to your room here. They want a brief interview that they can run on their evening news tonight. I didn't think you would mind. You're free, after that, until tomorrow's festivities."

"Okay, why don't you have the luggage sent up to my room. I won't be long, but I've got an errand to run. Important."

"Let me do it for you, sir. You must be exhausted after your long trip."

"No, no, I'm fine and I must do this myself. You go ahead and take care of things until I return and don't worry about me. I'll be back in plenty of time for that television interview."

After Sidney and my luggage had finally disappeared inside the Dorchester, I leaned forward toward my driver and asked, "What is your name?"

"Henry, sir."

"Henry, do you know a Matthew's Court, just a small street off Gloucester Place?"

"Indeed, I know it well, sir. I've lived about two blocks from there, in a small flat, since before the war."

"Great. Take me."

When the Marble Arch came into view, I could feel my stomach muscles beginning to tighten. How many times had I passed that lovely monument in Italian marble on my way to Winnie's place? At the arch we turned right and then left on Gloucester Place.

"Baker Street is just a short distance away, sir," Henry called out.

"Yes, I know. Is Sherlock still at 221b?"

He laughed. "You've been here before!"

"A long time ago, Henry, a long time ago."

Even the tiny doorways and iron balconies along Gloucester Place looked familiar. Total recall can be a terrible or wonderful asset. Finally the Rolls slowed and turned right. "There was once a sign on that corner post, sir, but this is it. Matthew's Court. What number did you say?"

"Twenty-two. It's on the . . . right . . . side."

Matthew's Court was a short dead-end street. On my left a three-story brick apartment extended to the street's end and turned, forming an L-shaped building. But to my right was nothing but mounds of bricks and stone and rotted lumber almost covered by tall, ugly weeds.

I opened the car door, and although the day was warm and humid I felt a sudden chill. I don't remember how long I stood, staring at the debris, before Henry's hand was on my arm.

"Begging your pardon, sir, but was this the address you wanted?" He nodded solemnly at the ruins.

I hardly recognized my voice. "The lady's name was Marlow. Winnie Marlow. Since you've lived in this neighborhood for so many years, did you happen to know her?"

He hesitated before removing his visored cap and wiping his brow. "No, sir, I can't say that I did, but I do remember, vividly, what happened here. Such a shame."

I inhaled deeply. "Tell me."

"I'll never forget it," he said, sighing and bowing his head. "T'was early on New Year's morning, 1945. One of the last German V-2 rockets scored a direct hit on the apartments on this side."

II

*J*ust five days after my twentieth birthday, in 1943, they pinned a pair of silver bombardier wings on my chest and presented me with a set of gold second lieutenant's bars. I was, according to Army Air Force decree, now an "officer and a gentleman" although I still couldn't vote.

That wasn't all I couldn't do. Following graduation from bombardier school, in Carlsbad, New Mexico, our class received ten days leave and I was probably the only graduate who didn't head for home immediately following the ceremonies. There was no home. I had lived with my uncle Pete since the age of eight, after that terrible night when the police came and told me that my mom and dad had both been killed on Route 9. A bus had lost control on the wet pavement, they said, and after the funeral I went to live with the only relative I had, just down the street from our apartment in Framingham, Massachusetts.

MISSION: SUCCESS!

Uncle Pete was a drunk, a mean one. When he was sober, which was not very often, he was always laying guilt trips on me about how he had saved me from becoming a ward of the state and how grateful I should be to him for taking me in and providing me with a roof over my head and a warm bed and three meals a day. What could I say? What could I do? I became his houseboy, mopping floors, dusting, making our beds, doing our wash, and I even learned to cook a little. The few dollars I earned from two paper routes, one in the morning and one in the afternoon, were scarcely enough to buy my clothes, especially since I was growing so fast. Naturally the kids at school caught on to my sorry predicament quickly, and kids being kids, they teased me unmercifully. Luke Gardiner was living with the town drunk.

Whenever Pete came home, after his almost nightly drinking binges at a local tavern, he did what came natural to him, I guess. He slapped me around after finding fault with how I had performed one of his assigned chores. I ran away four times, but the police always caught up with me and brought me back . . . so that I could get slapped around again.

I was a natural athlete, and by the time I was a high-school freshman I stood six feet tall, weighed 175, and Pete wasn't hitting me anymore. I wanted with all my heart to play football, baseball, and basketball, and Mr. Kearney, our math teacher who coached all three sports, did his best to convince me to try out for the teams. But I couldn't. I needed money for lunches plus my clothes and books, and Pete gave me nothing. So, instead of having my run at becoming a high-school hero, with the chance of earning a college athletic

9

scholarship, I went to work in the afternoons and all day on Saturdays at Flumere's Hardware Store.

In the evenings after dinner, which I usually ate alone, I began to spend my time in the nearby Merriam Public Library doing my homework. It was much easier to concentrate there, and I always felt comfortable and at peace surrounded by books. Since living with Pete, they had also become life preservers that I clung to desperately in order to survive an existence that no child deserves. Accidentally, one evening, I discovered that wonderful shelf of books on success and how to achieve it. I devoured Napoleon Hill's *Think and Grow Rich* and *Laws of Success*, William Danforth's *I Dare You*, Russell Conwell's *Acres of Diamonds*, and every Horatio Alger story I could find. What treasures! The more I read, the more I became convinced that I was not a loser condemned to a life of unhappiness because of conditions beyond my control. My destiny was in my hands, and mine alone, and soon I would be on my own with the power to change my life for the better. At last I knew I could endure any day because the future would be as bright and beautiful as I wanted to make it. What a revelation to a kid of sixteen!

I had a girlfriend. Her name was Priscilla Wheat, and, of course, she came from the affluent side of our small town. Why is it that the rich always live on the north side of town and the poor on the south? Priscilla's parents did everything possible to discourage our dating, but we still managed to meet at the library and take long walks together. I remember how ashamed I felt when I broke down and sobbed after confessing that I wanted to take her to our senior prom but I didn't have a suit. I had found a blue serge three-piecer in Penney's for only twenty-nine dollars, but when I asked Pete to loan me the money to buy it, he just laughed and kept reading his paper.

After graduation Priscilla went on to Wellesley College and I went to work in a local rubber factory where they were making inflatable rafts and life preservers for our armed forces. I earned forty-four dollars a week and Pete insisted that I turn over half of it to him to pay for my room and board. I did, without any argument, knowing that I wouldn't have to put up with him much longer since I now had a draft number and many of my former schoolmates had already been called.

One day Army Air Force personnel came to town and set up their recruiting stand on Framingham's small common. I enlisted after a young sergeant explained to me that the two years of college credits previously required in order to apply for cadet training toward becoming a pilot, navigator, or bombardier had just been lifted. All I had to do in order to take my first step toward earning my wings, he assured me, was to pass both a written and physical exam in Boston. If I failed, I would probably be assigned to gunnery school or one of the many ground crew jobs. Pete happily signed my enlistment papers, since I was under twenty-one, his only comment being that the army would probably make a man out of me.

I hitchhiked to Boston on the date set for my exams. An unsmiling corporal, before he passed out the written portion, announced that less than forty percent of the previous three groups had managed to meet the rigid Air Force standards necessary to qualify for flight training. Four weeks later I received official notification. I had been accepted and was to report to the National Guard Armory in Boston on December 10. Pete drove me to the railroad depot that snowy morning in his laundry truck. While we were waiting for the train from Worcester, he sat uncomfortably beside me in the small station saying nothing. When the train finally hissed to a halt outside, he reached into his pocket and said, "Here, Luke."

He placed five folded twenty-dollar bills in my hand. I stared at him, not knowing what to say. He muttered something under his breath and then I heard, "Take it. It might be a while before you get your first pay." Then we shook hands and he wished me good luck. As the train pulled away, he was standing alone on the platform, waving. I wasn't sure, but if I hadn't known better, I could have sworn he was crying. Pete wrapped his truck around a telephone pole three months later. I went to our base church when I received the telegram from his boss and prayed for Pete. There was no more I could do for him.

I wrote to Priscilla every day. My first letters originated from Atlantic City, where I suffered through all the tortures of basic training including daily marches up and down the deserted boardwalk in frigid temperatures while singing the Army Air Force song. The only bright side of those ten weeks was Glenn Miller. Major Glenn Miller. Since the army had taken over every hotel on the beach, we were not only living in them but also having our meals in what had been, prewar, elegant ballrooms and restaurants. Miller had just formed a service band and very often they played for us during our brief luncheon breaks. "Chattanooga Choo-Choo," "At Last," "A String of Pearls," "Moonlight Serenade" . . . whenever I hear a Miller recording now, I travel back in time.

One of my letters to Priscilla from Nashville proudly announced that I had qualified for bombardier training. After a rigorous screening program, some had made it for pilot training, others for navigation, and still others for bombardier school. I qualified for all three. Pilot training, they told me, would take at least seven months, navigation training would require four, and bombardier training only thirteen weeks. I opted for the quickest route to my wings and bars, fearing that if I dallied too long, I might miss the opportunity to fly combat against the Nazis or Japs.

A crowded troop train took us to the next phase of our training called preflight, in Santa Ana, California. The train trip lasted five days, traveling from Nashville via Biloxi and points west, including El Paso. To ease the boredom, since I didn't play cards, I kept a log of our trip and sent it all to Priscilla when we finally arrived in California, a thirty-seven page travelogue which she still has, although the ink has now almost faded away.

I went into Los Angeles only once during our Santa Ana stay. With three of my cadet buddies we hired a cab for the long ride into the city and found a small dive on Wilshire where Wingy Manone and his jazz group were playing. We all got very drunk and sentimental and lonely, spent the night in a small park on benches, and hitchhiked back to the camp in the morning. Joe DiMaggio was one of our physical training instructors on the base, but that didn't make seemingly endless push-ups, leg lifts, and stationary running any easier. They worked us as if we were preparing for hand-to-hand combat instead of the genteel life of a fly-boy. Palm trees and warm ocean breezes notwithstanding, we were all happy to say farewell to Santa Ana.

I was a member of the first advanced bombardier class to be trained in Carlsbad. After several weeks of heavy math and learning how to handle the top secret Norden bombsight in simulated bomb runs within a heavily guarded hangar, we began actual flights over the desert, two students to each plane plus a bored pilot. While one nervous cadet was dropping his five bombs on large white concentric circles of lime on the desert floor surrounding a wooden shack which was our bull's-eye, the other was leaning out a small hatch in the rear of the training plane, camera strapped to his wrist, recording each bomb impact. Then we would alternate. Back at the base the film was developed, each evening, and the number of feet we missed the bull's-eye on each bomb drop was recorded. Before we completed our training, we would drop fifty bombs, each carrying 100 pounds of sand plus a small flash charge that the camera would record on impact. If after the fifty bombs our total drop had averaged missing the bull's-eye by more than 230 feet, from 10,000 feet in the air, we did not receive our wings and commission as officers and were shipped off to gunnery school. "Washed out" was the phrase used for those who failed. My average was 139 feet, but fifty-two cadets didn't make it.

On the morning prior to our graduation, classmates in my barracks presented me with the golden cactus award, a scraggly prickly-pear cactus painted yellow, for "outstanding achievement." During one of my first bomb runs I had accidentally tripped the bomb release miles from the target area, so far away that the drop didn't count against my average. When I returned from that flight, the base adjutant and two surly-looking cowboys were waiting for me. It seemed that my errant bomb had killed two prize steers while they were grazing. The Air Force would reimburse the ranchers, I was informed; however, the total cost would be deducted, in installments, from my next six paychecks.

My printed orders, following graduation, commanded me to report to the air base in Salt Lake in ten days, where I would be assigned to a flight crew. We would then move on to a training base for two to three months of practice combat flying, as a team, until we were needed overseas.

And so, while my bombardier classmates all headed home to show off their wings to relatives and neighbors, in almost every state, I caught the first train for Salt Lake, checked into the Hotel Utah, and occupied those free days as best I could by writing countless letters to Priscilla, seeing all the movies in town, and spending much of my time in bookstores and libraries, still searching for answers, still trying to find the guidelines I needed to help me attain so much success that everyone back in Framingham, as well as in the rest of the country, would someday know who Luke Gardiner was and what he had accomplished with his life.

How could I know, how could I possibly imagine, that the answers were waiting for me, nearly five thousand miles away, locked in a safe in an apartment just off London's Gloucester Place?

III

When our bomber crew was finally assembled in Salt Lake City and flown to the air base at Casper, Wyoming, to commence combat training in the four-engine B-24 Liberator, we probably represented the typical cross-section of American youth that Ernie Pyle had been describing to millions of readers in his popular dispatches from the war zones.

Our pilot, Bob Lally, oldest crew member at twenty-six, was a high-school teacher from Lexington, Kentucky. Copilot Tim Ward had been a sophomore at Ohio State. Navigator Hank Mucci worked in his father's liquor store in Buffalo. Among the six enlisted men, four gunners plus an engineer and radio man, was a numbers runner from Brooklyn, an Oklahoma ranch hand, an accountant, two factory workers, and a kid just out of high school. Average age—twenty-three. Only Bob Lally was married.

None of us had ever even been inside an airplane in

civilian life, and now we were about to be entrusted with a huge and complicated carrier of death valued at more than 300,000 dollars. Sitting on its cement hardstand, the silver B-24 represented our nation's ultimate heavy bomber design. It towered more than 18 feet in the air, had a wing span of 110 feet, was 66 feet long, and weighed more than 50,000 pounds. Powered by four 1200 horsepower Pratt & Whitney engines, it was capable of delivering at least five tons of bombs more than 1300 miles and return, flying at 30,000 feet. The giant beast, glinting in the sun, looked indestructible, but we knew better. We all realized that it could become our coffin at any moment if the gods of war stopped smiling at us.

Three months later, in the spring of 1944, our crew had logged more than 200 hours in the air together. Since we understood how much our lives depended on each other, on each man doing his job well, we had flown practice bombing missions at dawn and at midnight, without complaint, navigational jaunts as far away as Seattle, countless gunnery sessions, instrument landings, low-level skip bombings, flights on three engines, tending to wounded on board, and even abandoning our plane after it had been badly hit, without actually bailing out.

Finally we were ready. Or at least we thought we were. Ten young men, not so far from their teen years, were now a combat crew, and since we had been hearing rumors that Ike was about to invade Europe, our only fear was that the war would be over before we saw any action. It was a wonderful age of innocence. We loved our country, and there were no marching picket lines creating doubts in our minds with chants of "Hell no, we won't go!"

One morning, early, we were awakened and told to be packed and ready to move out by noon. With three other bomber crews we were flown, in an old army transport plane, to Kansas City, Kansas, where a shiny, mint-condition B-24J, fresh from the factory at Willow Run, was assigned to us. After posing for the obligatory crew photographs in front of our new plane, we followed Bob Lally into a small briefing room.

Holding a brown envelope in his hand and smiling, Bob waited until we quieted down before saying, "Gentlemen, this is a great day. They must have liked our work at Casper because they're sending us to the big leagues! We've been assigned to the Second Air Division of the Eighth Air Force and we'll be on our way to England in the morning!"

He waited for the cheers to subside. "I m very proud to be a part of this crew. We have no weak sisters in this bunch. Now, if you're thinking about celebrating in Kansas City tonight, let me warn you that we leave at six-thirty in the morning and I want every one of you to be bright-eyed and bushy-tailed. Show up with a hangover and you'll be sorry you did. Our first destination is Dow Field, near Bangor, Maine. There we will receive our orders and flight plan to England, which undoubtedly will be over the northern route . . . and a lot of very cold water."

Tim Ward playfully pushed Hank Mucci's hat off. "Now we'll find out what kind of a navigator we've got, guys. If he blows it, we're all going to have an unforgettable swim."

Our crew training continued on the plane's maiden

voyage to Maine. While Hank labored down in the nose, his maps spread out on a small table, constantly giving directional corrections to pilot and copilot, our radio man, Gene Bonn, was also receiving fixes on our position from ground stations while I was sitting up in the nose turret checking our location visually with the help of pilotage maps. When we passed slightly north of Detroit, Hank's calm voice on the intercom announced that our estimated time of arrival, our ETA, was 1302 . . . two minutes past one in the afternoon. We touched down at Dow Field at 1304!

Any elation over having completed the first leg of our journey successfully was quickly dampened. It seemed that the oil pressure on our number three engine had begun acting crazily over Lake Erie and a decision was made by the base chief mechanic, after a lengthy consultation with Bob and Tim, to take the engine down and check it thoroughly. That meant, we were told, that we'd be around for four or five days before we could take off again. Then we were informed that we were confined to the base for the length of our stay since we were now on combat orders.

I phoned Priscilla early in the evening from the officers' club. It had been over a year since I had held her, and I missed her more than ever. She was home from college on Easter vacation, and I poured more than five dollars in quarters into that pay phone. She said she would pray for me and promised to write every day and I kept repeating, over and over, how much I loved her. The jukebox was playing "You'll Never Know" when I rejoined Tim and Hank at a corner table.

Hank slid a mug of beer toward me. "Come on, Luke, we're already three up on ya."

We drank in silence. Even talkative Tim just stared at his beer between sips. Three kids who had never been very far from their homes had just flown a heavy bomber halfway across the country. Ahead was a trip over thousands of miles of ocean and ultimately, combat, six miles up, in the deadliest sky of all above Western Europe. And now the terrible letdown. Time out. Just park it and wait.

"Where's the skipper?" I asked.

"Where else?" Hank grunted. "He's back in the barracks, sitting on his cot, writing another letter home. And Luke, you're almost as bad. I just don't know what you two guys find to write about every day."

Tim waved his empty mug in the air. He was already beginning to sway a little. "Luke, doesn't your girl live close to Boston?"

"About twenty miles west, in Framingham, my hometown too."

"How far—from here?"

"I don't know. About two hundred miles, I guess."

Tim nodded slyly at me, his mouth half-open. Then he rose, hurried to the bar, and returned with a tray and six filled mugs. Hank picked two quarters from the table, went to the jukebox, deposited both, and hit several buttons. Perry Como began singing "As Time Goes By." We each killed two more mugs before Tim repeated his last question to me.

"How far is it from here to your girl, Luke?"

"About two hundred miles," I growled. "Why the hell do you keep asking?"

Tim was getting drunk. I guess we all were. He

turned to Hank, pointed his thumb back in my direction, and said, "Here's the hotshot who always has his nose in those success manuals when he's not writing letters to his girl. He even tries to get us to read those silly books, telling us that we'll never make anything of our lives until we learn the principles of success. And look at him! Those books aren't helping him one damn bit!"

Hank frowned. "I just ain't following you, copilot. Explain yourself."

Tim nodded and set his mug down with a loud thwack. "Okay, okay. Luke, tell me, didn't one of those success books of yours state that you can accomplish anything you want in this world, providing you want it badly enough and are willing to pay the price? You know, the one you made me read."

I nodded. "Yes, it's in Napoleon Hill's book."

Tim's eyes narrowed. "Now, isn't that one of those success principles you're always preaching to us about?"

"Yes."

"Okay, now, Luke, what do you want right now more than anything in the world?"

I was sorry as soon as I said it. "I'd like to see Priscilla once more, before I go to combat."

"There you are, bombardier," Tim shouted exultantly, raising both palms in the air. "What you want more than anything else in the world is to see your girl once more! Now, if you really believe that you can accomplish anything you want in the world, providing you want it badly enough and are willing to pay the price, why don't you go see her?"

"Tim, you're drunk," Hank mumbled.

"Maybe so, maybe so, but listen to me, you guys!

21

Here we are, a crew without a plane to fly for the next four days, at least. We're not going anywhere, and we've got no duties here. There's not even a roll call. We just sit and wait until they put that engine back together. Now, we flew over Bangor on the way in here and it's only a couple of miles away. Trains, I'm sure, must be running from Bangor to Boston. All Luke has to do is get on that train, go on down to Boston, spend a day or so with his sweetie, and then get back here before our plane is ready. No one will miss him and no one will even know he's gone except us."

"You're not only drunk, you're crazy," Hank said. "How's Luke going to get off this base without a pass? This is an overseas port of embarkation. Maximum security. Guards everywhere! And if he gets caught, God knows what they'll do to him. For sure they'll pull him off the crew and court-martial him. This ain't like cutting class at Ohio State, kiddo. That's a hell of a price to have to pay."

"Well, I certainly don't expect him to try to walk out the main gate. Let Luke figure all that out. If he believes in that success principle so much, let's see him prove it!"

I drained my beer, saying nothing. The trumpet of Harry James plaintively sobbing "I Don't Want to Walk Without You, Baby" filled the now almost empty officers' club. I felt Tim's hand touching mine. "Luke, I love you and I'm glad I'm in your crew and I think you're a hell of a bombardier. No hard feelings, chum, but I've got a hundred bucks that says you can't pull it off."

I reached out, shook his hand, and said, "You've got yourself a bet, fella!"

IV

*P*riscilla's dad sounded angry. His voice was hoarse and the words clipped. "Luke, do you realize what time it is?"

"Yes, sir, I do, and please forgive me. May I speak to Priscilla?"

"Again? I think she's asleep. We were all asleep."

"I'm sorry, sir, but this is very important."

Long pause, eventually followed by Priscilla's soft voice, more throaty than usual. "Luke, what's wrong?"

"Nothing, honey, nothing. I've just got a little surprise for you."

"What?"

"I'm coming to Boston! I want you to meet me, tomorrow at three, in the lobby of the Hotel Touraine."

"What?" she screamed.

"Lobby . . . Hotel Touraine . . . at three tomorrow."

"How come?"

I didn't want to worry her. All I said was that we

had just learned that our plane was disabled for a couple of days and so we had some free time before heading overseas.

"I'll be there, darling, I'll be there," she promised, and hung up.

My wristwatch read five minutes to midnight as I hurried from the officers' club back to the barracks. Hank and I shared a small room. Bob and Tim were next door. Hank was sitting on the edge of his bunk bed when I rushed in to grab a towel and my toilet articles.

"Luke, don't be foolish. You know Tim. He was only teasing. You'll get nailed and ruin everything for yourself. Forget it and go to bed, huh?"

I mussed his hair as I walked past and out the door to the nearby latrine, where I showered and shaved. Fifteen minutes later, nearly dressed, I was wrestling with my tie when the adjoining door swung open and Bob entered, wearing only boxer shorts. Legs spread wide, he stood, hands on hips, staring at me and shaking his head. I said nothing as I carefully worked the tie knot under my collar. In the mirror I could see Tim standing in the doorway, looking downcast and guilty.

Finally Bob spoke. "Tim just woke me with some sorry news, Luke. You're crazy, buddy, you know it? You're going to get your fanny in a very tight sling if you get caught."

I kept my back to him. "I'll make it, skipper. Don't worry. Be back long before you're ready to take off."

"I should turn you in right now, you know that?"

That I hadn't planned on. As our commanding officer, it certainly was his duty to report one of his crew about to go absent without leave while on combat orders. Men had been known to chicken out before on their way to battle.

I placed both hands on the dresser and bowed my head until I felt his hands on my shoulders. He turned me around gently, and smiled.

"Luke, I'm going back to bed and get a good night's sleep. So far as I'm concerned, you're safely tucked in your little cot here. You give Priscilla a great big kiss for me and make damn sure you're back here no later than nightfall, the day after tomorrow, okay?"

I returned his embrace, threw on my green officer's blouse with its silver wings and gold bars, took several swipes at my shoes, checked my wallet, rolled my trench coat and tucked it under my arm, and headed for the door. Hank ran ahead and opened it, bowed low, and said, "Have a good time, kid, and kiss her for me too."

I stepped out into the chilly darkness. Sixteen hours earlier we had taken off from Kansas City. I should have been exhausted, but the adrenaline was really pumping now. Less than an hour had passed since Tim had thrown down his challenge. There had been no time to plan my "escape" from Dow Field, and I had no map of the base to guide me. Our barracks, however, was on a slight incline, and I could see that most of the base lights were to the south. Behind me, to the north, were only a few buildings bordered by a grove of tall trees. A dirt road ran past my barracks toward the shadowy woods. I decided to follow it.

Lord, it was dark, like being in a closed closet. Heavy overcast. No moon, no stars. I stumbled again and again in the loose gravel, stopping, every now and then, dead in my tracks to reconsider the foolishness of my mission. But I had made a commitment in public and I couldn't back down now. It's another success principle that I've followed throughout my life. Always put yourself on the spot. Tell everyone what your goals are, leave yourself no room to cop out, lock all escape hatches, and then you can move in only one direction—forward! I inched forward slowly, with only an occasional spurt of flame from my Zippo lighter to guide me.

Eventually my eyes became accustomed to the night and I could see the pale road for at least twenty yards ahead as well as silhouettes of bushes and boulders as I passed them. At least an hour into my march I heard the frightening sound of a motor and turned to see bobbing headlights coming my way. I dove behind a thick pine to my right and sprawled motionless as a jeep containing two helmeted military police passed no more than ten feet away. I watched as the headlights continued on for only a short distance before the bright beams reflected off a tall chain link fence. Paydirt!

The jeep paused for several minutes at the fence, then turned and came back down the road. I remained flat on my stomach on a bed of pine needles until I could no longer hear the motor. Then I jumped up and ran as fast as I could toward the fence.

The rusty metal links rose at least fifteen feet into the air, and on the fence top I could faintly see several strands of tightly strung barbed wire. Not knowing how much time I had before that jeep made a return trip, I rolled my trench coat tightly into a ball and stuffed it into the front of my blouse. Then, because my leather-soled shoes would hinder my climb, I removed them, tied the shoelaces together, and hung them around my neck. The ascent was painfully slow, a few links with each push, but at last my fingers touched barbed wire. I paused to catch my breath and then reached out with my right hand until I had a firm grasp on the metal brace holding the ugly wires. Using the brace as my only support, I pulled myself up carefully until I was balanced precariously on the top tubing that framed the fence below. Luke Gardiner and his "high wire" act! Slowly I raised one stockinged foot until it was over the barbed wire and resting again on the tubing. Then, almost as a pole vaulter would do, I shoved down on the brace, threw my other leg over the spiny wires, and plummeted to the ground. Thankfully, moist and tall grass broke my fall. I climbed to my feet, pausing only long enough to put on the trench coat and shoes before racing swiftly away from the fence before my friends with the black helmets reappeared.

Now I was in some sort of meadow or pastureland heavy with the pungent odor of cow dung. Advancing at a full crouch in an almost futile attempt to avoid stepping in any droppings, I pressed forward, praying that I would soon come upon a road of some sort. Just before dawn an old milk truck loaded with heavy aluminum containers clanked by within a hundred yards of me.

Once I was on the paved road, heading in the same direction as the truck, I realized for the first time that my shoes and socks and the bottom of my pants were soaked from the swamplike acreage I had left behind. And I was cold, trembling cold. Springtime in Maine! Soon I heard a rooster crow, and then another responded and the first orange rays of morning flashed to my right. I'm not sure, but I probably walked another two or three miles before I saw a lovely sight—a farmhouse with light shining from within!

I brushed myself off as best as I could, and praying that there was no unfriendly dog patrolling his turf, I walked up the driveway and knocked on the front door. Seeing my uniform, the tiny old man in loose overalls invited me in without hesitation. I was on my way to Bangor, I told him, when my car broke down, and I wondered if he'd let me use the phone to call a taxi since I had to be in the city by eight o'clock. Instead, he phoned for me, gave the dispatcher explicit directions to the farm, and while I waited he served me scrambled eggs, hot muffins, and sausage. Over our coffee we chatted about the war and Hitler and our Air Force until the cab arrived. Forty minutes later, just as the sun rose fully above the horizon, I was at the Bangor railroad station.

Despite the early hour, the old building was crowded with milling service personnel, each lugging a duffel bag or suitcase. Three military police passed through the crowd, checking papers randomly. I hurried to the ticket window, looking neither right nor left, and purchased a round-trip ticket to Boston. Since I now had more than an hour before departure, I decided that the safest place for me to wait was in a locked toilet in the men's room, so I bought a large paper cup of coffee, a doughnut, and a *Reader's Digest* and sat in there, on a very hard seat, until five minutes to eight. Then I slipped out, headed for Gate Four, and boarded the Old Boston & Maine train, trying to look calm and purposeful, as all officers should.

The ticket seller had told me we would arrive in Boston at two o'clock. Now I felt completely drained, and my good sense told me to stretch out and nap. But I couldn't. The thrill and excitement of the past few hours had me completely strung out. While the train rattled noisily through the soggy brown countryside, I finished with the *Reader's Digest* and then began on a discarded *Boston Post* that had been on the empty seat next to me. Then, at least one hour out of Bangor, my heart did a flipflop. An Army military policeman and a Navy shore patrol person had entered our car from the one just ahead and were passing down the aisle, checking every serviceman's papers. I was trapped and there was no place to hide and no toilet to lock. The two moved slowly and deliberately through the car, carefully checking each individual's orders and asking a question or two before passing on. I thought of Priscilla, patiently waiting in the lobby of the Touraine as the hours ticked by, three o'clock, four o'clock, five o'clock, and I could just hear her parents when she returned home, heartbroken, and told them that Luke had stood her up. Damn! I had almost pulled it off!

Now they were close. I forced myself to open the *Post* to the sports page and tried to concentrate on an article describing Ted Williams's Navy duties. I raised the paper higher, as if it would protect me from my fast-approaching doom.

"Good morning, sir." The army man wearing the black armband with the letters *MP* smiled at me over the top of my paper. The navy man also nodded pleasantly.

"Good morning," I croaked.

"Heading home, sir?"

V

"Dummy!"

I was staring at the bathroom mirror and realizing that in my haste to get off the base I had forgotten to bring my shaving kit. Luckily I had a pocket comb, but finding the other toilet articles in a drugstore would have to wait. My watch read two minutes to three.

With her coat folded loosely over her arms, Priscilla was standing near the hotel's glass revolving door and staring out at the noisy traffic on Boylston Street. I started to call her name as soon as I stepped off the elevator, but instead I walked up behind her on the thick carpeting, reached around her head, and covered both her eyes. Without uttering a sound she placed both her hands over mine and held them there for several seconds before she drew my right hand down to her lips and kissed it. Then she turned, her eyes filled with tears, and we embraced.

Finally she stepped back and said, "Let me look at

you!" She touched both gold bars on my jacket and softly caressed the silver bombardier wings.

"My hero," she murmured, shaking her head. "God, you look wonderful in that uniform. I can't believe that you and I are standing here, touching each other."

I kissed her again. "You know what I keep telling you, hon. You've got to start believing in miracles . . . and this really is one."

First we went to the drugstore on the corner of Boylston and Tremont, where I stocked up on the toilet articles I had forgotten to bring. Then we hurried back to the Touraine and up to my room and I showered and shaved in record time, finishing just as room service delivered two large hamburgers, french fries, and chocolate milkshakes.

Between mouthfuls Priscilla did her best to bring me up-to-date on our mutual high-school friends as I called the roll.

"Steve Tota?"

"Steve was going to barbers' school, but he's just been drafted. I don't know where he is."

"Mike Clemons?"

Her face clouded. "Joined the Marines. Dead on Guadalcanal."

"Phil Watson?"

"In the Navy. Was home about a month ago. The *Framingham News* interviewed him."

"John Reese?"

"Working at the country club. I think he's 4-F. Always has his father's car, with plenty of gas, and dates everyone he can."

"Paul Mazinski?"

"Killed in Italy . . . at a place called Salerno."

"Marty Cousins?"

"He's home now. The last time I saw him he said he'd rather be dead. Is on crutches. Lost a leg in the invasion of Sicily."

"Bill Tarcher?"

"Deferred. Sole support of his mother or something like that. Is engaged to Ruth Larosa."

"Frank Orcutt?"

She lowered her head. "Air Force. Bombardier. The papers said he was . . . missing . . . in . . . action over the . . . English Channel."

I changed the subject quickly. Ever since I had known her, Priscilla had always worn her pale blond hair in shoulder-length curls, but now it was very short. "Why did you cut your hair?"

"I just got tired of looking like Shirley Temple. And besides, if I had known I was going to be seeing you again so soon, I would have left it alone. Now you tell me something, Lieutenant. If you're on the way to combat, how did you manage a pass to come down here? Dad says that's very unusual."

I confessed everything, beginning with Tim's challenge back at the officers' club, and by the time I had finished, her blue eyes were opened very wide. "My God, Luke, what if they catch you when you try to get back on the base? What will they do to you?"

"I don't know. Probably arrest me and pull me off the crew. Maybe some sort of court-martial. But don't worry, honey, I made it out and I'll get back in, somehow. And it was all worth it, believe me, just to be with you for even five minutes."

"Luke, how long has it been since you've had any sleep?"

I had to stop and think. We had taken off from the field in Kansas City at six-thirty yesterday morning, seven-thirty Boston time. Now it was almost six-thirty in the evening. "I guess I've been awake for about thirty-six hours."

Priscilla sighed, pushed back her chair, and walked over to the bed, removing both pillows from under the bedspread. "You come on over here and put your head on this pillow, right now!"

"I'll be okay. We've got so little time together, I don't want to waste any of it sleeping."

She pounded one of the pillows with her open palm. "Right now! Come here and I'll rub your forehead."

"I want to take you to The Beachcomber tonight."

"It's still early. Come and rest for a couple of hours and you'll feel so much better. Please."

She lay next to me on the bed and we kissed . . . and kissed. Finally she pushed my chin back until my head was almost buried in the soft pillow and panted, "Now, you stay put and close your eyes."

Her hand felt so cool and soft on my forehead. . . .

When I opened my eyes, Priscilla was propped up on her right elbow, staring down at me. She leaned forward and kissed my nose. "Hi, sleepyhead."

I yawned and stretched. "What time is it?"

"Just a little after midnight."

"Oh, no! Why didn't you wake me? I had such great plans, and now everything is ruined. Damn! Damn! And what about your folks? Won't they be worried, knowing you're with me?"

"I've already called them. Told them I was spending the night with you and you were leaving in the morning."

"And your father is driving in to rescue you, right?"

"Dad was asleep. I talked to Mom."

"And?"

"She sends you all her love."

I reached up and pulled her head down to my chest. "Priscilla, when I get back, will you marry me?"

She moved up until our lips were touching. "You know I will. I want you with me forever, Luke Gardiner. I love you so very much."

It was as simple as that. In less than a minute we made a lifetime commitment to each other and celebrated our engagement by taking a cab to Chinatown and gorging ourselves on spare ribs, shrimp fried rice, and several glasses of wine.

Just before three in the morning we returned to the hotel. My train back to Bangor had a seven o'clock departure time. No sense in trying to sleep now, so we lay on the bed, fully clothed, and talked until dawn about our future together. When I returned from the war I would take advantage of the new G.I. Bill and get that college education I had once believed was hopeless. It would be rough for a while, but I could always get a part-time job while going to school, and Priscilla was certain she could convert her degree from Wellesley into a well-paying job. Of course we'd have to be careful about having children until we could afford them, but we could wait. How easy it all seemed at age twenty. Life, we were both confident, would be just what we wanted it to be provided we tackled it together. Together! That was the key word.

She rode with me to North Station. Then she would stay in the cab and go to South Station to catch a train back to Framingham. As our cab slid under the elevated lines in front of the old terminal, I removed the bombardier wings from my blouse and placed them in her hands.

"Wear these for me, please, until I can buy you an engagement ring?"

One final kiss. I watched as the cab pulled away, fighting back tears without much success.

When my train arrived in Bangor, I managed to squeeze myself into one of the three waiting cabs, along with five others, positioning myself up front next to the driver. "Drop me off last," I said softly, and he just cocked his eyebrow and nodded. We toured most of Bangor, delivering the other fares, and when we were finally alone, I asked, "Is there a back way to Dow Field where I might have a fighting chance of getting in without getting nailed by the guards?"

He chuckled. "Most of them are trying to escape, but you want to break in?"

"It's a long story."

"I'll bet it is. Sure, I think I know a way. No guarantee, though."

After passing miles of potato fields being plowed for spring planting, we turned onto a small dirt road overhung with bushes and tree branches, and eventually stopped at a clearing littered with tin cans and paper trash bags.

"This is as far as I can go and still turn around, Lieutenant. Just follow the road for about another quarter of a mile and you'll come to the base fence. It's a tall one, with barbed wire on the top. And a patrol goes by every thirty minutes. Are you sure you want to risk it?"

I tipped him and nodded. "I'll be okay."

The chain link fence and even the barbed wire proved to be much easier to handle in daylight. Luckily this time I kept my shoes on, because I landed on my feet, inside the base property, before rolling over. In the distance through the pines I could see smoke curling up from rows of barracks.

Bob and Hank and Tim were all sitting on my bed playing poker when I pushed open the door. They dropped their cards, leaped up, and cheered. I went over to Tim, extended my hand and said, "Pay up, buddy, one hundred bucks!"

Tim grudgingly counted out five twenty-dollar bills, all the while shaking his head. "I can't believe you made it, I just can't."

I reached into my blouse's inside pocket and handed him the dated paid receipt for one night's lodging at the Hotel Touraine, and then had the last word as I intended.

"Tim"—I grinned—"do you know the greatest difference between people who are failures and those who are a success?"

He scowled and shook his head.

"Successful people do the things that failures are afraid to tackle."

VI

Just before noon the following day, our wheels lifted off the bumpy runway at Dow Field. The first leg of our North Atlantic journey to England would take us to the American air base in Greenland, more than fifteen hundred miles away, bypassing the usual initial stop at either Gander or Goose Bay. No other bombers accompanied us.

Less than thirty minutes after takeoff Bob solemnly announced over the intercom that the United States border was now behind us and we were flying over New Brunswick. No one responded with any wisecracks. The fun and games were over.

Our plane was not equipped with the famed Norden bombsight, that marvelous electronic aiming device that had finally made daylight bombing a successful reality for our Air Force. It would be installed at our final destination. Since I wasn't needed for visual navigation until we approached the coast of Greenland, I propped up my parachute as a pillow near the bombardier's front Plexiglas window with its panoramic view, and let the constant moan of the four engines lull me to sleep.

Paul's voice in my earphones awoke me four hours later. "Hey, bombardier, how do you like those icebergs?"

The altimeter near my left elbow indicated that we were flying at only eight thousand feet above sea level, as per our flight plan. I yawned, rolled over on my stomach, and looked down at the gray Labrador Sea, speckled with whitecaps. No land was in sight. Instinctively I turned to make sure that my orange Mae West was still hanging on the bomb bay handles. Silly. None of us would survive for more than ten minutes in that frigid water. Dead ahead were at least a dozen towers of ice floating side by side.

"They look like giant chess pawns, skipper," I replied, "but wait until you see Greenland. I remember reading that more than eighty-five percent of the island is covered with a permanent icecap and the ice at its center, almost two miles in depth, has pushed the land down until it's more than a thousand feet below sea level. Greenland, they say, looks like a long narrow bowl of frozen milk."

"Luke?" It was Tim's voice.

"Yeah, Tim?"

"You're too smart for a bomb dropper. Here's one for ya. We've got a big yellow moth up here in the cabin and the critter has been driving us nuts ever since we left Bangor. Bob says it's bad luck to kill it, but I think we'd be doing it a big favor if we did. When we land in Greenland and open the doors, he's going to fly out and he won't know where in hell he is. For sure he's never going to see Bangor and his old moth friends ever again. Tell me, O great reader of books, should we put him out of his misery?"

Before I could reply, the familiar voice of our tail gunner, George McCord, spoke out. "Leave him be, Tim. He's no worse off than the rest of us. If you stop and think about it, there are ten other moths in this plane. We don't know if we're ever going to find our way home either."

We landed in Greenland just before 2200 . . . 10 P.M. The midnight sun was still shining, and an hour later, as I was crawling under three heavy blankets, it had just begun to set. It would rise again, they told me, in less than two hours. I didn't wait up for it.

Refueled, we departed early in the morning for Meeks Field, Iceland. Because of low cloud cover, we flew most of the thousand miles without ever seeing the ocean, but Hank's navigation was perfect. The young corporal who drove us to our quarters told Hank that the base officers' club was one of the best anywhere, but we were too tired to investigate. On the following afternoon we landed at one of our air bases in Northern Ireland, where our plane was taken from us. New B-24J's, we were informed, were issued to the various bases on a "need" basis and the group to which we have been assigned, the 475th, was not on the list. After a long and dismal bus ride we boarded a steamer, crossed the choppy Irish Sea in the rain to Liverpool, and then rode an ancient train across the belly of England, eventually arriving at a small railroad station called Marley Junction feeling mean, exhausted, and hungry.

Our base, named after the nearby village of thatched-roof homes, Marley, was one of fourteen B-24 bomb groups in the Second Air Division. The First and Third Divisions flew B-17's. Together, the three divisions, including fighter groups, made up the Eighth Air Force in England, occupying more than sixty airfields in an area smaller than Orange County, California.

Our bomb group, the 475th, and the other thirteen in our division, were all clustered in fields around the city of Norwich, in East Anglia, which someone had aptly renamed "Little America." We were approximately twenty miles from the English Channel, a hundred miles from London, and a hundred and twenty miles away from Nazi-occupied Belgium . . . twenty-four minutes by air!

Unlike our sterile airfields in the United States, which were usually built on worthless land as far as possible from civilization, the British bases had been hastily erected for us, with American supplies and money, on the only ground available—precious farmland—and the farms, for the most part, continued to function. Cows and sheep grazed placidly behind our officers' club, haystacks were piled everywhere, even alongside the runways, and fields of wheat and barley and cabbages grew behind our living quarters, separated from each other and us by deep ditches and hedgerows.

In this sylvan setting nothing could have looked more out of place than the hundreds of half-round, corrugated iron Nissen huts, scattered everywhere, which housed the more than three thousand personnel required at each base to perform all the menial, boring, difficult, and often dirty jobs necessary in order for the flight crews, that small and exclusive glamour set, to take their Liberators out on bombing strikes, day after day, weather permitting. Still, there were few working at any sort of ground duty who envied the crews their privileged status and probably none who would have changed places, even for a day, with those "crazy, young kids" who never knew, when they awoke, whether or not they'd still be alive at nightfall.

On the morning we arrived at Marley we were greeted at headquarters by group adjutant, Major Petrie, in his small office. He shook our hands after returning our salutes, asked us to sit, and welcomed us to the base. Like all adjutants, he was smoking a pipe.

"Gentlemen," he said, tapping his briar into a wastebasket, "we're pleased to have you as part of this great group and we know you will be a credit to the 475th. Your driver will show you where the officers' mess hall is located, the briefing room, and the quarters where your enlisted men will be billeted. There are three squadrons on this base. Yours is the 736th, commanded by Captain John Joyce, who will be in touch with you later, when he returns from today's mission. Your base commander is Colonel Roger Allen, and you will meet him eventually. The finance officer is right down the hall, in case you still have any American money that you want to convert to British pounds or have any questions about your pay. Lieutenant Lally, we'll always contact you regarding practice missions, and it will be your responsibility to notify the rest of your men as to time and other details. If you gentlemen are smart, I would advise you to buy yourselves bicycles as soon as possible. It's a hell of a hike to the mess hall and the briefing room from your quarters, and you'll find bikes for sale everywhere, especially by crews who have completed their missions and are awaiting orders to go home."

Tim raised his hand. "Major, how long before . . . before we see any combat action?"

"Depends on how good you are. Three, maybe four practice missions. A week if the weather stays good. We've got to be certain that you know how to get yourself into group formation upstairs, with thirty-five other planes, without running into anybody. Gets a little ticklish when five hundred planes from fourteen fields take off before dawn and they're all circling around in a small expanse of dark sky trying to find the rest of their group. But I'm sure you guys will do fine. By the way, have any of you spent any time in Nissen huts before?"

We all shook our heads.

"Well," he said with a grin, "it's not the Waldorf, but it's still better than sleeping in a muddy foxhole and I'm sure you'll adjust fine."

Major Petrie wasn't kidding. Our Nissen hut was not the Waldorf or even the Shady Lane Motel. Inside a metal structure, perhaps thirty feet long and ten feet high at its peak, were sixteen cots, eight jammed up against each of the two side walls. One small window at each end was covered with a dusty blackout curtain.

Our young driver carrying two of our duffel bags gestured toward four cots that were naked except for thin, yellow-streaked mattresses. "Those are yours, gentlemen. Make yourself at home while I bring in the rest of your stuff."

At the center of our hut was a thin cast-iron stove from which a sooty smokestack extended up through the curved ceiling. Black smoke seeped out through the top lid, and we were all hacking and coughing within minutes.

"My God," cried Hank, "what is that?"

The grinning private said, "That, gentlemen, is your source of heat. I guess somebody tried to burn some wet wood this morning, before they went to briefing. I hope you all have long underwear. Gets a mite chilly in here at night, even at this time of the year."

"Where is everyone?" Tim asked.

"On a mission, sir. Maximum effort today. Thirty-six planes. Munich."

A gray-haired orderly delivered blankets and pillows to us while we were unpacking, and we set about the almost impossible task of trying to make our small living areas tolerable. One of the first things I did was unpack Priscilla's framed picture and set it on the small nightstand next to my cot. We were nearly finished when we heard the roar of engines approaching.

"That must be our guys coming home," Bob exclaimed. "Let's go outside and watch."

The ground trembled beneath our feet when the first squadron passed low overhead. "I count eight," yelled Tim above the din. "Should be twelve."

The next squadron circled near us. Seven. In the final squadron, eight.

"Look at all the red flares! Wounded aboard! And there's one with his tail half gone and two engines out. Dear God!"

We finished unpacking in silence until the other residents of our hut began straggling in, one or two at a time, each pausing to introduce himself to us rookies. They all looked exhausted and no one was smiling, but one tall bombardier did tell us that we had four lucky cots. The previous occupants had completed their tour of duty, thirty-five missions, and had departed for the States the day before.

We four were getting ready to hike to the mess hall when there was a knock on the door, and a blond captain, who had been dozing in the end cot, rose and opened it. Two bespectacled corporals, both looking old enough to be our fathers, said a few words to the captain in low tones before he nodded and pointed to the four beds directly across from ours. We watched, completely innocent of the drama that was taking place before our eyes, while the two carefully removed all items, photos, and clothing from the footlockers and nightstands near each of the four cots, and placed them carefully in four separate bags. Then they thanked the captain and were gone.

I was sitting at the foot of my cot, staring at the captain, when he turned in my direction. His voice cracked, but he forced a smile. "You'll have to get used to that, kid. Those four great guys won't be sleeping here tonight. Had twenty-four missions under their belt, but a big fat eighty-eight shell nailed them on the bomb run today. Direct hit. Got themselves scattered all over Munich. Special Services will send their personal stuff home in a cardboard box after their folks get a telegram from the Secretary of War."

Later I turned to Hank and sighed. "Well, old buddy, let's go get some chow."

Hank shook his head and continued staring down at his hands. "You go ahead, Luke," he half-whispered, "I'm not hungry anymore."

VII

"*P*eople of Western Europe. A landing was made this morning on the coast of France by the troops of the Allied Expeditionary Force. This landing is part of the concerted United Nations plan for the liberation of Europe. . . ."

General Eisenhower's terse radio announcement to the world, on the morning of June 6, 1944, came as no surprise to us. Having completed our practice flights and been officially okayed for combat duty, we flew our first mission on D-Day as part of the giant air armada that dropped thousands of tons of explosives on the beaches of Normandy in advance of our landing crafts and barges.

By month's end we had five missions under our belt and all of the cockiness we possessed when we left home had slowly drained away. The average life of a bomber crew, in the summer of '44, was approximately twenty-one missions, and yet our tour of duty called for us to fly thirty-five. Tough odds!

Following each mission, every crew was interrogated by our group intelligence officers on all details of the trip, especially if it had been a rough one. On our fifth, a nightmarish and costly strike against oil refineries near Hamburg, the flak, exploding anti-aircraft shells, had been so thick over the target that we even resurrected that old line about there being enough of it to walk on, and after leaving the target area we had been attacked by enemy fighters.

Five of our planes were destroyed and the double shot of whiskey we were served, after landing, was scarcely enough to sustain us through the interminable questions ranging from the nose colors of the attacking Focke-Wulfs to how many parachutes, if any, we had seen escaping from our falling planes.

"Lieutenant Gardiner?"

I was stumbling out of the debriefing hall, alone, when I heard my name. Captain Small, our group personnel officer, was hurrying toward me accompanied by an elderly man in green fatigues and combat boots wearing a press pass and carrying a fat notebook.

"Lieutenant, I have someone here who wants to meet you. This is Phil Peters of the *Boston Daily Record*. Familiar with the paper?"

"Of course. Been reading it since I was a kid."

"Well, Mr. Peters is doing a series of articles on Massachusetts men in combat, and when we went through our records this afternoon, he selected you. Do you suppose you could spare him some time for an interview? I know you must be exhausted after that ordeal today, but it shouldn't take very long and Colonel Allen would appreciate it."

The reporter's handshake was firm but his voice was soft. "How do you do, Lieutenant. I know this is a terrible imposition, but I promise not to take too much of your time. What we're doing are personality pieces that will help bring this war closer to those back home so they will appreciate and continue to support people like you who are fighting so bravely."

Captain Small nodded. "The kind of stuff Ernie Pyle does, Lieutenant, you know—"

Peters interrupted. "Ernie does a wonderful job, but we're concentrating on the men from our state exclusively. An article about you would certainly make your folks proud, at the very least."

I started to walk away. "My folks are dead."

"I'm sorry. Didn't know that. Well, your girlfriend, perhaps?"

Without exception, I had written to Priscilla every day, usually only a few sentences on V-mail, to reassure her that I was still alive and well. Although her letters constantly pleaded with me to share what I was going through, I didn't want to worry her and so I restricted my combat news to how many missions I had flown and how many more I had to fly before we'd be in each other's arms. Officers were permitted to censor their own mail, but we were still subject to spot checks and even though I had been tempted more than once to spill my guts to her, my notes usually covered only the lousy weather, terrible food, and how much I loved her.

"Okay, Mr. Peters, let's do it."

It was still early at the officers' club. Two hours from now they'd be four deep at the bar, trying very hard to forget Hamburg. We settled into a worn sofa near the unlit fireplace, and during our first two beers moved to a first-name basis while I gave him a quick rundown of my early years as he filled several pages in his notebook.

"Cripes," he gasped, "you're not even twenty-one yet, are you?"

"I will be in five months or so . . . on December twelfth, although I feel a lot older than that tonight."

"Luke, let's talk about these combat missions, and please don't worry about security. Everything is censored before it leaves London, okay?"

I nodded.

"How long was the actual flight today?"

"About seven hours."

He shook his head. "And when did you first know you were flying this one?"

"They closed this bar last night at eight o'clock. That's our first clue that the group has been put on alert for a mission except that none of us ever know which crews are flying, so we all climb into bed early."

"It's gotta be tough trying to sleep with that on your mind."

"I did my share of tossing and turning . . . and wondering . . ."

"Wondering?"

"If I'd be alive tonight."

"Do you pray?"

"To my mother. I figure if anybody is in heaven, she is, and so I kinda ask her to pass my prayers on."

"Interesting. So when did you know you were going on today's mission?"

"When a little man with a clipboard and a flashlight

awoke me and told me that briefing was in forty-five minutes, at four-thirty."

"Does anybody ever groan, turn over, and fall back to sleep?"

"They wouldn't dare. Too proud. Instead, we really move our tail. First we dash to the latrine, about a hundred yards away, for a shower and shave. Then we dress, just about any way we like so long as it includes long underwear, and ride our bikes in the blackout to the mess hall."

"Why do you bother shaving, Luke? Who cares if you have a stubble on your face five miles over Germany?"

"If we didn't shave, the oxygen mask would cause a terrible skin rash in that sub-zero weather."

"Is the food good?"

"It was this morning. Usually we're served those awful powdered eggs with our greasy sausage or bacon. But today we got real eggs and ham, our first hint that this mission was going to be no picnic."

"After breakfast, what?"

"We walk to the briefing hall to learn our fate. At the door, two MPs check our dog tags before admitting us. Rumors have been floating around that German agents dressed like us have been sneaking into our briefings lately and radioing our mission destinations back to their fatherland."

"That's new," the old boy said, writing rapidly. "I've often wondered, what goes on at your briefings?"

"Well, the smoke in that damn room is thick enough to cut. We all find seats and wait. At exactly four-thirty someone in the back yells 'Ten-hut' and we all jump to our feet as Colonel Allen and his staff walk down the aisle toward the small stage. Our colonel is not one for small talk. After asking us to be seated, he turns the briefing over to Major Landers, our intelligence officer. Behind the major is a large map of Europe covered with a blue cloth. On a signal from him the cloth is jerked away and we all groaned and moaned this morning when we saw our target. A strand of heavy red yarn attached to the map with tacks ran from our base to the coast, across the Channel to a point north of Amsterdam, and then almost easterly across Germany to Hamburg, our target. Our return route, after the bombing, was over the North Sea and then south to England. A tough and long mission."

"Luke, how did you feel right about then? Scared?"

"Damn right. We all are but we try not to show it."

"Does anyone give you a pep talk, like a football coach before the big game, or perhaps to try to calm your fears?"

"There's always a chaplain around in case you want to talk, but there's usually no time for that. In the next fifteen minutes we learned more than we wanted to hear about the large number of anti-aircraft guns protecting our target and the possibility of encountering enemy aircraft before and after we drop our bombs. If we are hit badly and don't believe we can make it home, we were told to make a run for Sweden, where we would be detained until the war is over, which sounds enticing right about then. After we were briefed on the weather for the entire route, Colonel Allen wished us a safe journey and we all performed the usual ritual of synchronizing our watches with him."

"How cold does it get up there?"

"When we reach our maximum altitude of twenty-five thousand feet, it will be around fifty below."

"How do you dress for that?"

"I'm a bombardier but I'm still flying in the nose turret as a gunner. Since it's an awful tight fit for me, in the turret, along with two fifty-caliber machine-guns, I wear a thin electric suit under my brown gabardine flying outfit and leather jacket. Once I have eased myself into place after takeoff, I will plug my suit into a socket and hope it still works as well as it did when I checked it on the ground. Also, I will hook up an oxygen mask to my face when we reach twelve thousand feet. Without oxygen, above that height, one is usually dead in twenty minutes."

Phil Peters shuddered. "What about a parachute?"

I smiled. "There's no room to wear it in the turret. I just toss mine under the navigator's desk and hope that if we're hit, I'll have time enough to escape from the turret and clamp it on before I jump. Easier said than done, especially if the plane has its controls shot away and goes into a steep dive."

"Luke, I'm puzzled. If you're a bombardier, why are you flying as a nose gunner?"

I sighed. "Good question. During the early days of this air war, our planes would attack a target one at a time, with every bombardier doing his thing. But now, as the number of bombers has grown, each squadron of twelve planes drops its bombs together in formation, which greatly improves our chances of hitting the target. Only the bombardier in the lead plane and the deputy flying on his right wing now have bombsights. The deputy will take over only if the lead bomber has been knocked out of action. The rest of us just follow the leader, and when he drops his load, so do we. Before I complete my tour of duty, Phil, I expect to be flying lead bombardier. I know I will! I didn't spend all those months of training and come halfway around the world just to push a bomb-release button."

"I believe you, son, I believe you. Now, what about those takeoffs before dawn? Aren't they dangerous?"

"That's always sweaty-palm time for everyone. We knew we were carrying a heavy load of bombs and gas today, and the runways here are not that long. Only last week one of our planes had not been able to get airborne before reaching the end of the concrete strip."

"What happened?"

"Ten guys dead and there's now a large black hole in what had been a field of brussels sprouts, just beyond the runway."

"Was it close today?"

"I swear our right wing clipped some tree branches this morning."

"Luke, what I've never been able to understand is how you guys get into such tight formations up there, in the dark, before you head for Germany."

"Well, it's a miracle to us too. There are thirteen other groups, all from nearby fields, also trying to form up there. Our group leader takes off first, and as he climbs he begins to fly a prearranged circle path, firing flares as he goes so that his other crews can find him. Each plane, when it finally makes contact with the leader, slides into an assigned spot, and the group keeps circling until everyone is in formation. Usually takes an hour or more."

"But isn't it pitch-black? How do you keep flying

formation, with wings almost touching one another, in the dark?"

"Actually it's more gray than black, up there. We can see silhouettes of the other planes, but it's still the toughest part of any mission, and we all breathe a sigh of relief when we finally head for the British coast and our group falls into line with the other groups. There have been many collisions up there."

"Okay, now you're on your way. What next?"

"Once we are over the channel, as the ship's armorer I tell all gunners to check their guns and the plane shakes while the guys each fire a few bursts into the water below. Then we settle back for a long ride, our eyes constantly searching the sky for trouble."

"And you've got an up-front ringside seat!"

"I sure have. It's a fantastic sight from the nose turret. At altitude, all our plane's engines are spewing out a trail of white condensation, and if your group is flying back in the line, it almost looks like a white highway in the sky. Soon after we hit the enemy coast this morning, we were joined by our 'little buddies,' several groups of P-47's and P-51's flying protection for us. That's also a lovely sight, believe me!"

"I heard this was a rough one today. When did the trouble begin?"

"It was a breeze until we got to the target area. No flak and no enemy fighters. But as soon as we reached the point where the bomb run began, all hell broke loose. From the initial point of the run, when we open our bomb bay doors, usually twenty or more miles from the target, the pilot of the lead plane switches to automatic pilot, which is connected to the bombsight in the nose. During the bomb run the lead bombardier is steering his plane. When he adjusts his crosshairs in the sight, the plane responds by turning right or left as he turns his dials, and the rest of us just follow him, still in formation. Now, during the bomb run the enemy knows we must fly a straight course; their radar has charted our exact altitude, and it is also obvious what our target will be. They respond by firing a steady barrage of eighty-eight and hundred-and-five millimeter shells that explode in clusters directly in front of us, knowing that we must fly through this wall of death in order to release our bombs on target. Also, some of their guns are tracking us, firing directly into our squadron."

"And there's no place to hide."

"There's no place to hide and there's no place to park it if you get in trouble. It's the most helpless feeling in the world. You're sitting there, surrounded by thin Plexiglas, seeing nothing but big ugly puffs of black smoke ahead, and you think there is no way any of the planes will escape through that box of exploding shells. Down below I could see bright orange balls of fire and a lot of smoke, so I knew that the groups ahead of us had already scored hits on the refineries. Finally we were in the middle of the flak and a plane directly in front of us suddenly exploded with a huge flash of light. We went into a dive to avoid the debris just as a body sailed directly above my turret. To my left, a wing floated lazily down, its rear edge burning. We finally regained formation just in time to release our bombs with the others and the squadron turned as quickly as it could away from Hamburg toward the North Sea."

"Was your plane damaged?"

"Our tail gunner, George McCord, reported that there were two gaping holes in the tail but, luckily for us, the controls had not been damaged. He also informed us that a second plane of ours had been hit, lost its right wing, and tumbled crazily to the ground. He saw no chutes."

"But your day wasn't over yet, was it?"

"Nope. Just as we left the German coast and headed out over the water, we were attacked from the rear by at least two dozen Focke-Wulfs firing cannons. George did yell that they were coming at us, but they blew through our whole group so fast that it was over in less than sixty seconds. Three more of our planes went down and thank God the FWs didn't turn and come after us again."

Phil had ceased writing and was staring at me. He lit a small cigar and asked, "Luke, are they all like you?"

"What do you mean, sir?"

"Well, you've just described what I can only imagine must be one of the most frightening ordeals any human should ever have to deal with, and yet you've done it all so clearly and calmly, almost as if you were describing a hike in the woods. Amazing! And I'm sure you've probably spared me a few gory details, and that's okay. But this was your fifth mission today, and that earns you and your crew an Air Medal. Do you feel like a hero?"

"Hell, no. There are fifty empty beds on this field tonight, and one of them could have been mine. All I know, for sure, is that we've now flown five . . . and we're still alive."

"Thirty more to go?"

"One at a time."

"Have you been to London yet?"

"Tomorrow afternoon. We're getting our first forty-eight-hour pass in the morning, I hope."

"Where do you plan to stay?"

"I don't know. One of the hotels around Piccadilly Circus, I guess. My schoolteacher pilot is going to Oxford, but my navigator and copilot have women on their mind."

He winced. "They'll find nothing in London but prostitutes . . . Piccadilly commandoes. And you?"

I shook my head. "I don't mess around, sir. I'm engaged and I love my girl enough not to ever cheat on her."

He tore a page from his notebook, scribbled a name, address, and some numbers and handed it to me. "Phone this woman tonight. Winnie has some very special lodgings in London, and caters almost exclusively to American flying officers. She'll charge you a little more than you would pay at the Regent Palace or some of the other places, but I believe you're the kind of person who will truly enjoy your stay with this very special lady. In fact, I guarantee it."

Before leaving the club I phoned Winnie Marlow, mentioned Phil Peters, and reserved a room.

It was the luckiest and most important phone call I ever made in my life.

VIII

*D*usk had already fallen on London, and despite our snaillike pace the taxi ride from Liverpool Street Station, in the blackout, had seemed as frightening as any combat mission. I overtipped my old driver for delivering me safely, found my way up the concrete steps to 22 Matthew's Court with the help of my trusty Zippo lighter and knocked on the heavy wood-carved door that opened almost immediately.

"What is it?" a female voice asked from the darkness.

"I'm Lieutenant Gardiner. I have a reservation."

"Oh yes, Lieutenant, we've been expecting you. Please come in and then we can close the door and give you some light. Must be careful with our blackout, you know."

I edged forward until I was inside. As the door closed behind me I heard a loud click, and a crystal chandelier directly over my head filled the marble-tiled hall in an amber glow. When I turned, a dark-skinned woman in a starched gray maid's uniform was staring at me, wide-eyed, her hands over her mouth. A soft moan escaped from between her fingers before she lowered her hands tentatively and whispered, "Who are you?"

"The name is Gardiner. I phoned Mrs. Marlow last night about a reservation. What's wrong?"

She shook her head violently. "N-n-nothing, sir, nothing. Kindly wait in the sitting room there, and Mrs. Marlow will be with you presently."

It was the kind of dream room I often fantasized having in a wing of that special home I would own when I achieved success. The walls were paneled in light oak with built-in bookcases filled with colorful leather volumes soaring higher than any human could reach. Above a stone fireplace hung a cluster of miniature oil landscapes each framed in thick gilt molding. Near the fireplace, alive with flames from a small gas unit, was a rolltop desk on which stood several framed photographs and a vase of fresh roses. I moved toward the books, wanting to get closer to them, to run my fingers over their textured leather bindings and read some of their gold-embossed titles, but instead, I settled into a high-backed chair near the desk, feeling very insecure and out of my league.

I stood and faced the doorway when I heard footsteps approaching and my hostess entered the room with a warm smile that faded immediately when she saw me.

"Dear God!" she cried, now advancing toward me at a much slower pace. She extended her right hand with obvious effort and inhaled deeply. "How do you do, Lieutenant. I'm Winnie Marlow and I do apologize for our rather strange behavior, both Martha's and mine. Doesn't make for a very cordial first-time welcome, I must say, but you look amazingly like someone we once knew. In fact, the resemblance is frightening."

She was tiny, probably little more than five feet tall, and wore a white satin robe tied loosely at the waist. Her gray hair was swept back in a chignon, and the large green eyes, studying me intently, were framed by high cheekbones, which were accented by a pert nose covered with freckles.

I shook her hand but didn't know how to respond. She nodded toward the seat I had occupied and slid back the cover of the rolltop desk, turning her chair so that she was facing me.

"I was expecting you this afternoon."

"We came down on the London and North Eastern Railway. The train was two hours late arriving at Marley Junction and then it took almost five hours to get here. Had some trouble with one of the drive wheels on the engine."

When she smiled, small lines curled around both sides of her mouth. "That's about par for the course. But I guess we should be grateful that the old system is working at all after these past four years. Lieutenant, you sound more British than American."

I grinned. "That's what the men in my crew tell me too. Was born and raised close to Boston. And you sound more American than British, Mrs. Marlow."

"I'm originally from Warren, Michigan. We should get along fine, young man. Would you like to see your room before you register? If you don't approve, of course you are free to go elsewhere."

Already I felt completely at ease with her. "I'm quite tired and I guess I'd be the happiest guy in the world, right now, with a warm shower and a comfortable bed."

"Very well. Two nights lodging, as I told you on the phone, is five pounds. And that includes breakfast in your room if you really feel like spoiling yourself. There is only one strict house rule which I hope that our mutual friend, Phil Peters, has explained to you. For two years now I've worked very hard to make this place a sanctuary, a haven where you boys who live with death every day can get away from that hell and relax in comfort, peace, and quiet. To me, all of you who risk your lives in the heavens are very special people and you deserve the best. However, although this city seems to have abandoned most of its morals, you are still not allowed to entertain any women in your rooms here. The nice girls are no longer in London, anyway, and I'll not be a party to any of you getting in trouble with prostitutes or contracting any disease that may haunt you for the rest of your lives. I'm really not old-fashioned at all, Lieutenant, but if you have any 'shack-up' plans, to put it as delicately as I can, then you should consider staying elsewhere. I hope you understand."

I laughed aloud. Felt good. "Mrs. Marlow, I'm probably more old-fashioned than you are. I happen to be engaged to the greatest girl in the world and I don't think I could ever face her again if I fooled around even once."

"Sign in, Lieutenant."

She watched as I completed the registration form. "Luke," she murmured, "that's a marvelous name. May I call you Luke?"

"Please."

"And I'm Winnie, okay?"

We shook hands again. "Luke, I see you're with the 475th group. How is Colonel Allen these days?"

"Busy. I'm proud to be in his group. You know him?"

"We're old friends. While he was flying his combat missions he stayed here often. I knew him when he was only a captain, which doesn't seem that long ago. And where are the other members of your crew tonight?"

"I have no idea where the enlisted men have gone. My pilot is in Oxford, soaking up culture, and our copilot and navigator went to the Regent Palace Hotel in Piccadilly Circus. They were told that the downstairs bar there is a great hunting ground."

She nodded. "Only problem is that your friends are the prey, not the hunters."

I shrugged. "They're big boys."

"Of course. Men of the world. And they deserve all the fun they can find since they don't even know if they'll be alive next week, right?"

"Sounds familiar. Roman gladiator stuff. Eat, drink, and be merry . . ."

She was staring at me again. Now there was a hoarseness in her voice. "Come, and I'll show you to your room."

Carrying my suitcase, I followed her up a winding stairway to the third floor. At the top of the landing she removed a key from her pocket, unlocked the door marked 3A, and ushered me into a suite that would have made General Eisenhower envious. Oriental rugs, several of them, accented the highly polished dark wood floor in a room that seemed large enough for a football game. Oil paintings and exotic wooden masks hung in profusion on every wall, and next to the huge fireplace was a writing desk complete with stationery, a quill pen, and a crystal inkwell. Blackout curtains hung over the tall bay windows, but they were covered with delicate lace which swept down to a long curving bench seat covered in dark velvet velour. Against one of the walls was a filled bookcase and a floor model Atwater Kent radio. The bathroom, with its separate dressing room, was more spacious than most hotel rooms I had occupied, and its tub looked large enough to swim in.

"Well, Luke," she asked, "does it satisfy you?"

"Are all your rooms like this?" I gasped.

"Pretty much. There are seven others and I'd be happy to show you some of them but they're all occupied tonight, as they are on most nights."

"Air Force people?"

"Hundred percent. Seven Americans . . . and one Canadian. A good mix. The British boys usually head for home when they get leave, which is where they should be. With their families."

A yellow terry-cloth bathrobe lay at the foot of the bed. She pushed down on the quilted spread. "Goose-down mattress and Irish linen sheets, Luke. After those hard cots, you should sleep well tonight."

"It's so quiet here," I said sighing. "No planes are warming up or racing their motors. Day and night, it's a sound you learn to live with, I guess, back at the base. But you never get used to it. It's always there in the background, reminding us that there will be another mission tomorrow . . . and the next day. . . ."

She touched my arm gently. "We've paid a high price for this stillness, Luke. Goering and his air force did their best to keep us awake almost every night for quite a spell, and I'll never forget it. There's a good part of London that is still ashes and rubble. Now, tell me, what would you like for breakfast?"

"Gosh, I don't know."

"How about some orange juice, pancakes with honey, sausage, and coffee with real cream?"

"You're kidding! I'd love it. You must know the Prime Minister?"

"As a matter of fact, I do. What time would you like your food?"

"Is ten too late?"

"Not around here. And what are your plans for tomorrow?"

"I thought I'd go sight-seeing with the guys. Stuff from our history books . . . you know . . . Big Ben, London Bridge, Westminster Abbey, the Tower of London. . . ."

"Very good. See you in the morning."

She stood on her toes and kissed my cheek before leaving. I undressed and let the hot shower run until my skin had turned a deep pink, dried myself with a giant, fluffy towel, and fell into that glorious bed, naked. As soon as my head nestled into the soft, clean, sweet-smelling pillow, I was fast asleep.

The high-pitched wail of a siren sounded as if it were right outside my window. I fumbled for the lamp switch and sat up in bed, wondering if it had been a dream. The sound continued, and now I could hear other sirens in the distance. There hadn't been a bomber raid on London for almost two years. What was going on? The terrifying alarm continued, and I didn't know what to do. Winnie hadn't briefed me on this. Hurriedly I slipped on the yellow robe and raced to the door, flying down the circular staircase two steps at a time. Just as I reached the hall, Winnie appeared from a room to my right.

"What's that all about?" I asked breathlessly.

Her voice was calm. "It's probably one of Hitler's latest gifts for us. Haven't you heard about the madman's new toy, buzz bombs? They commenced arriving about two weeks ago and there's probably one somewhere over the city although I can't hear it. Sorry, I should have prepared you."

Of course I had read about Germany's new secret weapon, the V-1, pilotless small planes loaded with a ton or so of explosives that were now being launched at England. Before I could reply, we heard a muffled explosion far off, and the sirens ceased.

"Has London been getting hit with many of them?"

"Three or four each day and perhaps a couple at night. Just remember, Luke, you're safe as long as you hear that dreadful doodle-bug's motor. Only when it cuts off does it begin its downward glide path until it hits something."

I tried to smile. "That's very reassuring, Winnie."

The lines curled around her mouth again. "Were you asleep?"

"All the way."

"You know, I never even asked you. When did you last eat?"

"Breakfast, I guess. There was no dining car on the train, and in all the excitement about coming to London, I just forgot to get hungry."

Her lovely laugh sounded like notes on an ascending musical scale. "Come into the kitchen, poor child, and

I'll whip you up a sandwich. I'll even find you a glass of fresh milk."

Winnie watched with unconcealed pleasure as I stuffed myself. Afterward, as we walked to the foot of the stairs, she said, "Luke, I must explain to you why Martha and I acted so queerly when we each got our first glimpse of you this evening. I owe you that much. Will you please indulge an old lady and come into the sitting room again for just a minute?"

I tightened the belt on my robe and followed her over to the rolltop desk. She removed one of the gold-framed photographs from its top and handed it to me. "This is a photo of my only child, Dana. He was a fighter pilot with the Royal Air Force. Spitfires. Three years ago, during a German air raid, he was shot down right over this city."

I was now staring at a young man dressed in his RAF uniform that proudly displayed his pilot's wings. I raised the picture closer to my eyes and blinked. I looked again. No way! Impossible! But there it was. The face in the frame, smiling up at me, was mine!

IX

*T*he sumptuous breakfast that Martha wheeled into my room promptly at ten was delicious, and I savored every morsel. Another new experience in my life. Room service! Afterward I lingered over my third cup of coffee and lazily leafed through the pages of *The Times* feeling more like royalty than like a small-town kid far from home. If this was a taste of success, I knew I wanted more of it.

I dressed in slow motion and went downstairs. Fortunately Winnie's sitting room door was ajar and I could see her busily writing at her desk. I knocked softly, asked for permission to use her phone, and called my buddies at the Regent Palace. The disappointment must have been showing when I finally dropped the phone back on its cradle.

"Something wrong, Luke?"

"I guess that Hank and Tim are in no condition to

go sight-seeing. They've both got roaring hangovers and have decided to spend the day in bed."

"Rest and recuperation so that they can attack London again tonight?"

"I guess."

Winnie rose and came toward me. Even I could appreciate the beautifully tailored light blue linen suit she was wearing. Unlike last evening, her face had a flush of color.

"And now what are your plans for the day?"

"I don't know. Guess I'll go wander around London anyway."

"Would you like a guide? I'd be more than happy to show you some of our city, that is if you can stand the company of an old lady."

"I'd love it, Winnie, but I couldn't ask you to go to all that trouble."

"Luke, what if I told you I had been planning on it?"

"What?"

"I suspected that your friends might be in no condition for city-hopping today, so I cleared my calendar just in case you needed me."

I hesitated. "Why are you doing this for me?"

She turned away. When she spoke, her voice was almost a whisper. "I'd be doing very little for you, Luke, compared to what you'd be doing for me."

The photograph of her son, Dana, was staring at us from the top of her desk. What could I say?

"Okay, lady, let's go!"

Like most American boys, I had an ongoing love affair with automobiles even though the fastest form of transportation I had owned in my civilian days was a second-hand Columbia bicycle with balloon tires on which I had delivered my newspapers. Winnie's car, parked at the curb, was the most seductive piece of automotive sculpture I had ever seen. I circled the beauty twice, gently rubbing my fingers along the glinting metallic-brown finish.

"What is it?" I almost moaned.

"It's a rather new breed," she said proudly. "Designed and manufactured by a couple of old friends of mine who have been building excellent automobiles here for years. Their first version of this lovely monster was produced in 1936. It's called a Jaguar, and this 1939 version is a drophead coupe—convertible to you— capable of going much faster than I've ever asked it to travel."

"Wow!" I shouted as I settled myself into the soft leather seat on the left side and the growling motor eased us away. I reached over and touched her gloved hand on the wheel. "Winnie?"

"Yes, Luke?"

"I'm glad that Tim and Hank have hangovers."

She clutched my hand, laughed, and said, "I am too, Luke, I am too!"

Winnie Marlow was a marvelous guide, and I probably saw more of London that day than most members of the Eighth Air Force saw during their entire tour of duty in England. Riding on the left side of the roads in congested traffic had me bracing my feet against the floorboards on many occasions, but I soon grew accustomed to automobiles and buses that seemed to be heading directly for us only to eventually slide by on our right side.

We began our tour just a few blocks from the

apartment, at Madame Tussaud's Wax Museum. For reasons that no Britisher could fathom, Winnie explained, this had become the most popular attraction for all visiting GIs, even surpassing Big Ben, London Bridge, and the wildest sections of Piccadilly. We gawked at the hundreds of amazingly lifelike wax statues of the famous and the infamous, including Roosevelt and Hitler, before we were back in the Jaguar and soon passing the tree-lined Baker Street home of Sherlock Holmes.

We stopped in a vacant parking lot near the towering Marble Arch while Winnie fussed over a few levers until the convertible top was lowered with my muscle. Now we could hear the infinite and discordant sounds of man and the city blending with the chirping of hundreds of birds from the greenery of Hyde Park, directly in front of us.

"This is our largest public park, Luke. It's been that, more or less, for over four hundred years. This place has seen it all, the best and the worst of our people and their habits. In there you will find a pet-dog cemetery, a bandstand, a birdwatchers' sanctuary, and a speakers' corner where anyone can mount a soapbox and speak on any subject he or she chooses. God knows how many duels have been fought here through the centuries, and old Henry the Eighth once stocked it as his private preserve for deer chases. In there you'll also find a statue of Peter Pan, an Italian garden, a street called Rotten Row, the wreck of an old gunpowder storage barn, a bowling green, and a putting green. You could spend a week right here and not see all this old park has to offer."

Whenever we approached any site that Winnie considered important, she would slow the Jaguar to a crawl, ignore the honking traffic behind us, drive close to the curb, and deliver the landmark's history to me in capsule form. We attracted more than our share of attention from passersby, especially American servicemen who stared in awe at the sleek convertible and were probably wondering how a lowly lieutenant managed to find a girl with a car like *that*. By now Winnie was wearing a silk scarf to keep her hair in place, and wide sunglasses, so no one could be sure from even a short distance whether my companion was twenty or sixty.

We laughed our way around Hyde Park Corner, paused at Buckingham Palace, Scotland Yard, Big Ben, and 10 Downing Street before easing into the congestion of Trafalgar Square, with its bold and hungry hordes of pigeons noisily fluttering around the tall stone column bearing Admiral Lord Nelson on horseback. What was a navy man doing on a horse? Winnie didn't know. Eventually we found ourselves on a narrow street filled with small shops, leading us to a wide cobblestone square.

"This is the heart of Piccadilly Circus, Luke, where all your lads seem to congregate. That boarded-up structure covered with posters in the center of the square was erected to protect the statue of Eros from the bombings, and even though it's still early in the afternoon you'll notice that the steps surrounding the covered sculpture are already quite jammed with soldiers waiting for adventure and romance to pass by. This would seem to be the perfect place for a statue to the goddess of love, but when it was erected, around the turn of the century, Eros was officially the angel of Christian charity. Rather ironic, what? Now, right up

Regent Street there, is the hotel where your friends are staying. Would you like to pay them a visit, perhaps bring them some packets of seltzer powder for their aching heads?"

"Let them suffer," I yelled over the traffic noise. "I've never had so much fun in my life and I'm willing to keep on as long as you are."

She smiled impishly, shifted gears, and soon we were on Waterloo Bridge, crossing the barge-choked Thames River. We slowed at the bombed ruins of the Old Vic Theatre, turned at St. George's Cathedral, and headed north until we were crossing the Thames again.

"Do you know what bridge you're on now, Luke?"

I shook my head.

"Shame on you. I'm certain you sang about it when you were a young lad."

"London Bridge?" I cried out, leaping from my seat and grasping the top of the windshield in order to get a better look. London Bridge! And it was not falling down, falling down, falling down!

Leaving the old bridge behind, Winnie turned right, and I could tell by the sun at our backs that we were headed east. We rode for several miles before the Jaguar reduced its speed, but this time my tour guide remained silent. Words weren't necessary. On both sides there was nothing but desolation. Now Winnie shifted into low gear and we crept slowly past block after block, completely leveled except for a ragged and lonely chimney here and there, dusty monuments to the families who had once lived in neighborhoods now vanished. It was a sight that I would never forget.

Winnie's dark green eyes were moist when she said, "The Germans destroyed more than a million homes in this city during the blitz, Luke, and at least half a million people perished from the bombs and fires. These were the slums of London, where large families were packed into dingy tenements. Most of the bombs fell here because it's so near the Channel and they say there are ashes of hundreds of bodies out there mixed with the cinders of ceiling beams, floors, and cheap furniture. The terrible fires that always followed the bombings lit up most of London night after night, and one could feel the heat from the flames miles away. Most of your friends, unfortunately, don't get over this way, but I wanted you to see some of what we've had to endure. Hitler has no idea how close he was to victory when he suddenly decided to change his tactics and ease off on the bombings."

Later, over sandwiches and tea in a crowded restaurant near the Tower of London, Winnie leaned forward and said, "Tell me about Luke Gardiner." For the next hour, with gentle prodding plus a well-placed question every now and then, she had me rambling and reminiscing, and there was little she didn't know about me by the time I had finished.

She started to refill my empty cup from our third pot of tea. Instead, she set the pot down, clasped my cup in both her hands, and raised it until the china was close to her face. "Have you ever had your tea leaves read, Luke?"

I chuckled. "No."

"I'm quite good at it. Would you like me to read what I see for you?"

"Only if it's good news."

She peered into the cup for several minutes, frowning. "Amazing! I've never ever seen these patterns before. How strange . . . and yet how wonderful!"

"Will I complete my missions in one piece?"

"You will, and when you return home, you will marry Priscilla as you are planning to do. Then I see many years of hard work and struggle, eventually leading to more success and achievement than even you dare dream about. Someday you will be one of the wealthiest and most powerful individuals in the world."

"Rags to riches, huh? A real self-made man?"

"Self-made? No. You will have had much excellent guidance along the way from a very special source, a source available to all of mankind but rarely tapped because of our ignorance and blindness."

She had lost me. I shook my head, baffled.

"I'm afraid I'm racing ahead of you a bit, Luke. You see, I've learned to look upon life as a mission that each of us must fly on our own. What they teach us in school helps us only to get off the ground, but we'll certainly never arrive at the targets of our dreams unless we learn from those who have completed successful missions before us. Tell me, Luke, in all that reading that you've done, have you spent much time with the Bible?"

"No. I can remember going to church and Sunday school when my mom and dad were alive, but I couldn't understand why God let them die when I was only eight, and I'm not sure I understand even now. I'm afraid I'm not very religious."

"Well, you can relax because I'm not going to preach any sermon to you, but are you familiar with the biblical person called Paul?"

I shook my head.

"Paul was a tough and gutsy little guy who became convinced that his life was a special mission, to sell his faith to the world beyond Jerusalem. He did a marvelous job of it, too, traveling from city to city, but he soon learned that after he had departed a place for a certain time, the people he left behind would begin to backslide into their former miserable way of living. So, while he continued with his mission, he began writing letters back to them, exhorting them with countless reasons filled with logic why they should hold to the truth as he had taught them. I tell you about Paul only because in one of his many letters he wrote about that special group of people who had passed on but by their example, their actions, and their words had left behind a priceless legacy for all to share. Paul refers to these unique individuals who had fulfilled their missions of living a good and fruitful life, despite all sorts of obstacles and handicaps, as 'clouds of witnesses,' witnesses to a happier and more successful life, who still watch over us. I've given these special people another name."

"What do you call them?"

"Friends in high places—because that's what they are. Our friends. Our teachers, if you will. They may have departed from this earth last year or many centuries ago, for a higher place, but their principles for success and happiness are still alive, and if we learned and applied some of them to our own lives, we could achieve most any goal."

"These friends in high places, are they the source that your tea leaves showed would guide me on my mission in life to more success than I could possibly imagine?"

X

We ended our whirlwind tour at the Tower of London, strolling hand in hand through ancient grounds still enclosed by stone walls and a moat now covered with grass. To my surprise there wasn't just one tower, but many, and Winnie knew them all by name. There was the Wakefield Tower, Bloody Tower, St. Thomas's Tower, Byward Tower, Bell Tower, Middle Tower, Beauchamp Tower, Bowyer Tower and in the center, with four spires, was the tallest of all, the White Tower of Keep.

"William the Conqueror built that one," she said, "in the latter part of the eleventh century. The walls rise more than a hundred feet, and its silhouette dominated the London skyline back then, constantly reminding the king's subjects that they should think twice if they had any ideas about overthrowing their ruler. This was where royalty lived for many years and the crown jewels are still on display here. It has always served as a

77

prison, too, for those the powers considered dangerous troublemakers, people like Thomas More, Jane Grey, Sir Walter Raleigh, and Thomas Cromwell. Some of More's finest writing was done in there before he was finally beheaded."

I couldn't resist. "One of our friends in high places?"

She squeezed my hand. "Yes, he certainly belongs in that group. His ethics and moral code should prove invaluable to any young attorney or politician aspiring to great things. Just think, Luke. Right now we're standing on eight hundred years of history. Tourists come here to see the dungeons and the coronation crowns and the royal sceptre with its massive Star of Africa diamond, but the most precious jewels of England, and every other nation, are the seeds of powerful ideas and guidelines for a better life planted by people like More for everyone to share. Instead, most of humanity stumble through each day, blindly trying to reinvent a wheel that has already been created and used successfully. How sad."

Much later, with the sun still high because of double daylight savings time, we both hobbled wearily toward an empty bench near the Tower Green, where Anne Boleyn had been executed. We sat for several minutes, as close friends often do, without feeling the need to say anything, and I was slowly leafing through the pages of a small Tower of London guide book when I heard her exclaim, "Look, Luke!"

High above us, toward the west, a single-engine Spitfire with its easily recognizable elliptical wings was performing a series of graceful rolls and turns in the clear blue sky. "Isn't that a lovely sight?" She sighed.

When the silver bird finally disappeared behind the

buildings, tears were streaming down Winnie's cheeks and I wrapped both my arms around her small shoulders. "Hurts every time you see one, doesn't it?"

She nodded against my chest. "He was a wonderful son, Luke, and you not only look exactly like him but you *sound* like him. Dana was in his second year at Cambridge when he joined the Royal Air Force. We were so short of pilots in the latter part of '40 that they rushed him through flight training but that didn't faze him. On the day he received his wings he said that his one goal was to keep the damn Nazis from destroying his childhood treehouse in the backyard of our home on King's Road. He survived just five weeks. . . ."

"And the treehouse?"

She pushed against my chest. "You *would* ask that! *He* would too. It's still there, Luke, so far as I know. I sold the house soon afterward. Couldn't stand living there alone. That's when I decided to buy the place on Matthew's Court and rent the rooms to Air Force personnel on leave. Somehow it has made me feel closer to Dana, gives me the opportunity to play 'mother' to a houseful of young men, and it's kept me so busy there's been little time to feel sorry for myself."

"How long have you lived in England?"

"Thirty years or so. I met Dana's father at a cotillion ball in Detroit when I was nineteen. My crippled father, whom I had taken care of since I was a child, had just passed away, and I was at rather loose ends. Peter was a handsome young chemistry professor at the University of Toronto on some sort of exchange program with Oxford. We lived in Toronto for a year after our marriage before he brought me to London, early in 1914, because Peter was afraid that England would soon be at war and he wanted to be home to serve in any way he could. Well, he did. He was doing government work on cannon shell casings when his laboratory blew up. Dana was born three months after the tragedy."

"What did you do?"

"Cried a lot, but I soon realized that tears weren't going to be much help in paying the rent or feeding the two of us. Peter had a lovely old maid aunt named Sarah who moved in with us, bless her heart, and became a sort of nanny for Dana while his mother went out into the cruel world to earn a living."

"How old were you?"

"Twenty . . . no, twenty-one, and I had never worked for pay outside the home a single day of my life. Also, unlike this war, not even the defense plants would hire a woman. I had received four hundred pounds from Peter's company insurance fund, and since I couldn't find a job, I decided to make one for myself. I opened a small store on Cannon Street, near St. Paul's Cathedral, and spent nearly all I had to stock it with yard goods. You wouldn't know this, Luke, but the sewing supplies that a woman uses, things like patterns, thread, and cloth, are usually available only in department stores. My idea was to concentrate exclusively on servicing the sewing woman and offer her a wide variety of fabrics plus all the sewing advice, training, and encouragement she could handle. I had been sewing since I was a child, mostly out of necessity, but it was something I had always loved doing and so I took the big leap . . . after a good deal of praying."

"And what happened?"

"It was a success from the day I opened the doors for

the first time. Two years later I moved to larger quarters on Carter Lane, but I kept the first store and promoted my most able clerk to manage it for me. Within ten years I owned a chain of fourteen stores throughout London, and Golden Needle Limited had made me a millionaire . . . in pounds, not dollars!"

I shook my head in admiration. "That's the kind of thing I dream of doing someday, Winnie. Wow, what a success story! You had no business education or management training, not even any work experience, and yet you went out into that all-male commercial jungle and parlayed four hundred pounds into a million . . . in only ten years! Amazing! How did you do that?"

Those huge green eyes twinkled. "Anybody with a burning desire to succeed can do what I did and more. I learned that from the years of helping my daddy. He was a sportswriter for the *Detroit Free Press* until he ended up in a wheelchair from polio. Since he could no longer cover his beloved Tigers, he began writing and selling articles to magazines like *Liberty*, *Collier's*, and many of the pulps. I became his legs and spent countless hours in the libraries doing research for the pieces he wrote. It was a better education than any college could have given me. As time went on, Daddy began selling more and more of his articles to a magazine called *Success* which was published by a genius of a man named Orison Swett Marden. Since that magazine was devoted to helping people change their lives for the better, I began spending more and more of my time gathering facts on the principles that history's most successful people practiced in order to fulfill their missions in life. That's when I first began calling them 'friends in high places.' To me they were voices from have of our good times together are worth far more to me than all my possessions."

"How did you keep from going batty during the days when Dana was in school? That must have been a tough adjustment after all those busy years and hectic pace."

"It was easy. I just shifted gears and decided to draw on all those success notes that had helped me, plus my years of business experience, and write a book dedicated to my father which I, too, would call *The Seeds of Success*. I remember him telling me that he believed most of the self-help books with tips on selling or managing or becoming a success in general were not nearly as useful as they were advertised to be because they focused on one's outside world instead of the inner world. He believed that one's success and happiness depended on what the person contributed, not what he or she received, and this was all linked to one's self-esteem. At the time I didn't really understand what he meant, but when I finally made it in the business world, I realized how correct he had been. And so I began spending most of my many free hours in libraries, while Dana was in school, searching for additional answers from my friends . . . answers that would help anyone have a successful day *today*. If one could do that, the weeks and months and years would take care of themselves. But when I finally began writing the book, I made a startling discovery."

I was hanging on her every word. "Tell me, please."

"Well, I probably filled my wastebasket hundreds of times with discarded pages before I realized that the true principles of success and happiness didn't need hundreds of pages of wordy prose to back them up.

They could all stand on their own without any dramatic coloring or exciting examples that success writers often employ to hold the reader. That's when I decided to put the book idea aside and rewrite each of my seeds of success in very few words, using the simplest language I could. I was very proud of the finished product. Each of the seeds I selected concentrated on this day alone, following that old admonition of just trying to live one day at a time. But with one great difference! Just to survive the day is not enough. One must live it using every bit of potential that God gave us. And so my seeds are a very brief day-to-day set of guidelines on how to be a happy winner in life, and I'm positive they will work for anyone who dares to live them every day."

"Sort of a twenty-four-hour life plan?"

She smiled. "Yes, you could say that."

"Did you ever publish *The Seeds of Success?*"

"No."

"Why not?"

"I was saving them . . . for Dana."

XI

When we returned to the apartment on Matthew's Court, two flying officers were just emerging from the sitting room. Winnie greeted both of them with warm embraces before introducing me. A wide-shouldered captain with pilot's wings and three rows of ribbons shook my hand and asked, "Is this your first visit to Winnie's, Lieutenant?"

"First time, Captain, but not my last, I hope."

"How many have you flown?"

"Five . . . a long way to go yet."

He patted my shoulder. "You'll make it. We don't lose very many after they've joined Winnie's club."

Winnie quickly interrupted. "Luke checked in rather late last night, Perry, and we've been on the run all day, so I haven't initiated him into our special group as yet. How many more for you two? You must be getting close."

"Better than that, lady. We're finished! Angelo and I

flew our last mission yesterday and we're hoping to be back in the States within two weeks. But we couldn't leave England without seeing you one more time and thanking you again for all you've done. We'll never forget you or this magnificent place. Never! Some of our crew are throwing a party at the Reindeer Club tonight, but we'll see you again, for sure, before we check out. Nice to meet you, Lieutenant."

After the front door clicked shut, Winnie leaned against it and shook her head ruefully. "I'm afraid they've rather spoiled my little surprise, Luke, but so be it. Do you have any more free time, or were you planning a rendezvous with your friends this evening?"

"I'm not going anywhere. This has been such a fantastic day that anything I do out there now would just spoil it."

"Excellent! Come with me."

Her long and spacious library was a larger version of the sitting room in decor except that books were everywhere, many even stacked on coffee tables and sideboards. Dominating the room, above a white stone fireplace, was a huge oil painting depicting a single hand with open palm reaching out toward the viewer from a jet black background. Nestled in the palm of the hand was a tiny figure of a man and woman, but surrounding the two were many signatures that were obviously not part of the original painting. Winnie touched a wall switch and the canvas shimmered in the light from two ceiling lamps.

"I purchased that oil many years ago, Luke, while I was traveling in Venice. It's by a little-known Italian Renaissance painter, Camecho, and is titled 'The Hand of God.' The engraved brass plate at the base of the frame was my idea."

I stood on my toes and read the words. *"See, I will not forget you. I have carved you on the palm of my hand."*

She rested her hand on my shoulder. "Those are the words of the prophet Isaiah, and there are none more beautiful or reassuring in the entire Bible. One night, more than a year ago, four of your lads were in here chatting with me. They were all bright and charming and bubbling with life, and yet as I listened to them talking about the missions they had flown and the friends they had lost, I could sense how frightened they were beneath the laughter and bravado. I wanted desperately to do something, anything, to soothe their fears, and on an impulse I picked up a pen, handed it to one of the young men, and asked him to mount this footstool, reach up, and sign his name in the palm of the hand after he had read the words aloud as you have just done. Of course, the other three had to follow suit, and when they finished, I promised them that they would be in God's hand, not only for the remainder of their combat missions but for their far more important mission, later, of living a good and productive life. As you can see, it's grown into quite a custom around here. We must have at least two hundred autographs up there, and so far as I know we've never lost a signer, call it coincidence or luck or . . . whatever you will."

"What do you call it?"

"Faith. It's the strongest armor a human can wear. I remember reading a book by one of Britain's most brilliant scientists, a man named Rawson, who wrote about an entire British regiment serving through all the horrors of the First World War without losing a man because they had all memorized and repeated, several times a day, the words of the ninety-first psalm which they called the Psalm of Protection."

"They survived just by repeating the words over and over?"

"No, by *believing* the words they were saying. There was a time in my life when I knew the entire psalm but I can still remember fragments of it. *'Thou shall not be afraid for the terror by night . . . nor the arrow that flieth by day . . . a thousand shall fall at thy side, and ten thousand at thy right hand, but it shall not happen to you . . . there shall no evil befall thee . . . for he shall give his angels charge over thee, to keep thee in all thy ways. . . .'* "

"More friends in high places?"

"Oh, yes . . . and one special friend," she said, bowing her head toward the painting.

A thick fountain pen lay on the mantel. I removed its cap and said, "May I?"

"Of course."

Standing on my toes, I leaned forward and carefully wrote *Lt. Luke Gardiner* on the painting's small finger.

"There," I said softly, "now I'm protected."

"Only if you believe you are, Luke."

Although it was late June, there was a chilly dampness in the room, and with Winnie's coaching I managed to get a log fire going in the wide fireplace after several false starts. I didn't realize it at the time, but she began briefing me for my future, my life's mission, that very evening.

My tie was loosened and my shoes were off and I was staring at the flaming logs, completely relaxed, when Winnie said, "Luke, earlier today when you told me about yourself I couldn't help noticing how bitter you still felt toward your dead uncle, who had made life so difficult for you, whipped you, and constantly told you that you would never make anything of yourself. You must understand that many children grow up to be failures because some adult, usually a parent or teacher, told them over and over that they would never amount to anything. Once this terrible prediction of failure has been imprinted on young, impressionable minds, these unfortunate kids unconsciously spend all their lives trying to fulfill the negative prophecies made about them, and they never know why they keep failing at everything they try. For reasons we'll never understand, that didn't happen to you. You should be grateful to Uncle Pete, and later in your life you will look back on those sad days and be glad they happened, except for losing your parents, of course."

"Winnie, how can I ever be grateful for those terrible years? I even dreaded getting out of bed in the morning. When Pete wasn't yelling at me, the kids at school were teasing me or talking behind my back because I lived with the town drunk, wore clothes that were almost rags, and never had any money to buy things like the others. It was a nightmare. It was hell!"

She clenched her small fist and waved it at me. "Exactly! But you never crumpled under all those slings and arrows as most children would do. Instead, you began visiting the library, searching for answers to your predicament, and you found enough of them in the success books to give you hope. You didn't give up on yourself. You turned that terrible negative environment into a powerful motivating force. Call it revenge if you wish, but you decided that someday you would be rich and famous and everyone who had taunted you would know how wrong they had been about Luke Gardiner. Think about this. Isn't that the reason you let Phil Peters interview you? History is filled with the names of great people who grew up starved for a little praise. One of our friends, a nineteenth-century American author, Christian Bovee, once wrote, 'Words of praise, indeed, are almost as necessary to warm a child into a congenial life as acts of kindness and affection. Judicious praise is to children what the sun is to flowers.' Never forget that, Luke, when you have children of your own."

This was not the same jovial tour guide who had filled my day with joy and laughter, and I listened, fascinated, as she continued.

"When Napoleon was a little boy attending the military academy, one of his teachers made life miserable for the tiny tyke by constantly telling him how stupid and inept he was and that he was certainly doomed to a life of failure. On his deathbed this great general and leader of men was heard to say that he wondered if this mocking teacher from his youth, Herr Bauer, had ever learned what Napoleon Bonaparte had achieved in his lifetime. Think about *that*! How many of Napoleon's victories were gained just to prove an incompetent mathematics professor wrong? We all yearn to be appreciated for what we are and what we can become. If you remember that, you will appreciate the force that is driving you and put it to good use. You will also be able to apply this success principle to get the necessary cooperation of others by feeding their spirit with praise instead of criticism and insults. Another of our friends, William Shakespeare, wrote that 'our praise are our wages. One good deed, dying tongueless, slaughters a thousand waiting upon that.' Now, do you have a little better idea of exactly what makes Luke Gardiner tick?"

"I sure do . . . and I thank you. I'll make it, Winnie, but it's going to be rough. I've got no education, no training in anything worthwhile, and I'm about as poor as anyone can be. Also, there's no family to lean on."

At last she was smiling. "Son, don't look to me for sympathy, even if you are the spitting image of my boy. You are already very special to me, but you are blind if you don't realize how much you have going for you. I'll prove it to you. Let's take a quick inventory of Luke Gardiner and try to put a value on the assets you possess right now. Are you game?"

I nodded and she handed me a blank sheet of paper and pencil. "Now, I want you to put down, in dollars, your response to each of my questions. Ready?"

I nodded again.

"What's your good health worth? Go ahead, put down a number."

Pause.

"What's it worth to live in your great country?"

Pause.

"What's your freedom worth?"

Pause.

"How about your eyes? Would you take a million dollars for your eyes?"

Pause.

"How about your hands and feet? Five million? Ten million?"

Pause.

"That bright mind of yours. How much? Let's stop

XII

*A*bove the head of Hank Mucci's cot, hanging suspended from the corrugated metal ceiling, was a multicolored map of Europe mounted on plywood. On it we recorded the missions we had flown by sticking pins into the targets we had hit after returning from each raid.

During the seemingly endless month of July, five more pins were added to the map at Munich, Saarbrucken, Gotha, Ludwigshafen, and Bremen. There had been eight empty cots in our hut following our trip to Bremen, but except for several flak holes in various parts of our Liberator's anatomy, our crew continued to lead a charmed life.

I was still flying as a nose turret gunner, but that lowly status no longer frustrated me. Even the gripping fear that had accompanied me on the first few missions had now been replaced by a serenity that I didn't try to understand. Naturally both Tim and Hank suspected that my days in London were somehow the cause of my newly acquired attitude and coolness under fire.

The three of us were at the club, following the costly Bremen raid, when Tim began probing again. "Hey, Luke, when are you going to break down and tell us about London? Come on now, fair is fair. Hank and I have given you all the juicy details of our little sessions with London's wild women and yet you haven't said a damn word about what you did. Why are you holding out on us?"

Now it was Hank's turn. "I think he got lucky, Tim, and caught himself a gorgeous chick and he's just afraid that if she met us, it'd be curtains for him."

Tim nodded. "You're probably right. Poor Priscilla. But what I can't understand is the change in him since we got back. Now he's as loose as a goose before each mission and on the intercom, even over enemy territory, he's funnier than Bob Hope. What happened to you in London, Luke, some kind of miracle?"

"Whatever it was," Hank groaned, "I'd sure like some of it. I don't think my heart can handle twenty-five more if many of them are like today's. I can still see Berry's and Castillo's planes exploding on that bomb run and the poor kid who fell right past our right wing with his chute on fire. God!"

Except for Priscilla, they were my two closest friends in the world, and I wanted desperately to tell them about Winnie, but I was afraid they would laugh at me. How could I possibly make them understand that a wealthy stranger, old enough to be my mother, had taken me under her wing because I reminded her of her dead son? And how would they react when I told them that she had promised to teach me all I would need to know in order to deal with life and win when the war was over? Hank and Tim's world, as mine had been, was completely dominated with surviving their tour of duty, but already I was thinking five and ten years into the future and instead of worrying about tomorrow's mission, I was just counting the days until I could be with Winnie again. Still, I did owe them some sort of explanation, if only to get them off my back, so I told them about Winnie, my elegant room on Matthew's Court, our London tour, and our long discussions, leaving out any reference to "friends in high places" or signing my name in the hand of God.

When I finished, Tim was staring at me with disbelief. "That's it? You spent all your leave with an old lady and she showed you London and then you just sat and talked a lot? That's it?"

"That's it, I swear. Hey, how about you two coming with me next time? I'm sure I can get you both a room and—"

"No way!" they shouted in unison. "No way!"

I returned to Matthew's Court alone, on my second forty-eight-hour pass, early in August. When I phoned Winnie from the base to reserve a room for the following two nights, she asked, "Are you coming down to work or play?"

"What do you mean?"

"I mean are you coming to London to bar-hop with your friends or are you going to allow me to plant a few more seeds of success that you'll be able to harvest later?"

"If it's okay with you, I'd like to work."

"I'll be prepared, son."

And prepared she was for what she announced as "the world's first seminar on success." Back then I wasn't even sure what the word *seminar* meant.

"When this war is over, Luke," she patiently explained, "I expect we will witness the greatest education explosion in history. Teaching will move out of the churches and classrooms in order to satisfy the needs of legions of adults seeking the knowledge and techniques they feel they still need to lead a better life. Today only a few people with vision, like Dale Carnegie, are out there conducting adult classes, wherever they can rent space, on subjects like public speaking and getting along better with people, but you will see the day when thousands of experts from every profession will begin making their experiences and expertise available to others, for the price of a ticket, and these sessions will become commonplace in theaters and hotel meeting rooms everywhere. Since the word *seminar* has many definitions, among them 'a meeting for giving and discussing information,' that word or one very similar will probably be used to define such meetings where many will gather to learn more about their particular profession . . . and about themselves. And so far as I know, there has been no seminar on success anywhere as yet."

I waved my arms around the library. "You have a very small class, teacher."

"Yes, but the quality is very high, I believe."

Clasping her hands together, she rose and looked down at me. "Let us commence . . . and for openers, Luke, tell me whether you would rather be successful or happy?"

"If I were successful, I know I'd be happy."

She grimaced and said, "Not true . . . and please take notes. You will meet many people in your life whom the public acclaims as famous and successful and wealthy and you will learn, to your dismay, that some of them are the most unhappy humans you can find. If you could sit them down and force them to tell you the truth, they would admit that they stopped enjoying their mission in life on the day they looked back and realized that the price they had paid for success was much too high. Don't you ever buy that fancy platitude that tells us 'success is a journey.' That high-sounding phrase is a trap because it infers that we must struggle, at all costs, to arrive at the first plateau and then we begin struggling even harder to reach the next level and then the next and the next until they finally dig a small hole for us and lay us to rest in our last plateau. Luke, if you arrive at that first plateau happy and contented, you don't have to climb any further if you choose not to. Success is not a journey, but a destination, and when you stop climbing should be decided by how you feel about yourself when you go to bed each night. Are you familiar with the writings of Blaise Pascal?"

"No, I'm not."

"Pascal was a seventeenth-century French philosopher and mathematician, and although he died before reaching the age of forty, his writings still go to the heart of so many of man's weaknesses. Pascal reminded us that the major cause of our unhappiness is that we don't know how to stay quietly in our rooms. Even kings, he wrote, get bored with life and need to be entertained, and so long as we depend on outside forces for our happiness, we are wasting our time. Material success is not the most important goal in life. Another friend in high places, Solomon, with all his gold and treasures and concubines and accomplishments, cried that 'it was all vanity and a striving after the wind and there was no profit under the sun.' "

I closed the notebook in which I had been writing and looked up at her, puzzled. "I don't understand, Winnie. Are you telling me that my goals are wrong? Last month your tea leaves predicted a great future for me, more than even I dreamed about. But from what you've just told me, I've got a lot of misery ahead of me along with the good stuff."

That memorable laugh echoed through the library. "No, no, dear boy, there is nothing wrong with your goals. I'm just waving some red flags at you so that you will be able to avoid the traps that snare so many ambitious people. You have no obligation in this world to succeed, to become wealthy or famous, only to be true to the best you can be without always trying to top yourself while on an endless journey. You are familiar with Robert Louis Stevenson?"

"Of course. *Treasure Island* . . ."

"Stevenson once wrote, 'To be what we are and to become what we are capable of becoming is the only creed of life.' I just don't want you ever to lock yourself in some gold-plated office dungeon while the roses are fading outside your window. If you ever have to make a choice between one more late business meeting or dinner with your family, go home. There is nothing sadder than a millionaire, who always worked fourteen hours a day, walking past the rooms where his children once slept and wondering where they had gone. Remember my words, Luke, and those of Pascal, Solomon, and Stevenson!"

"I will, Winnie, I promise you."

She sat next to me and placed her hands on mine. "Can you be both successful and happy? Of course. Once you learn never to depend on outside diversions like titles or buildings or gold for the peace and satisfaction that can spring only from the tranquility and love you feel inside. No one understood Jesus when he told us that the kingdom of heaven was within each of us. I'm not so sure that we do yet. How sad."

XIII

*M*emories. My treasure chest is filled with them and very often the aging images from my combat tour of duty shift as swiftly in my mind as do the patterns in a kaleidoscope. . . .

Giant barrage balloons, each tethered by steel cables, floating by the hundreds over London to snare Nazi buzz bombs. Gene Bonn, our fun-loving radioman, whose laughter was stilled forever by a jagged fragment from an anti-aircraft shell during our fourteenth mission. The tiny lamb who, one day, wandered away from the grazing herd behind our Nissen hut and casually walked in to visit us. Our plane, trying to land without brakes after the hydraulic lines had been shot out, burying its nose at the end of the runway. The monthly dances at our officers' club, when buses of young ladies were brought to the base from nearby towns and it always took the MPs several days to round them up afterward. The ugly bombs, hanging in our bomb bays before takeoff, painted with every possible obscenity for Hitler. The green of England's countryside. The acrid smell of fifty-caliber bullets after they had been fired. The White Cliffs of Dover. George McCord downing three Messerschmidts with his twin tail guns on our twentieth mission. The proud sounds of Big Ben. Glenn Miller's mysterious disappearance over the Channel.

All my memories, however, are little more than faded tintypes when compared to the permanent imprint that Winnie Marlow left on my mind, my heart, and my life. She was determined that I would complete her seminar on success before my combat tour had ended, and so each of my visits to Matthew's Court during the months that followed were intensive training sessions that often continued far into the night. I loved every minute of them, filling countless notebooks with priceless information on living and achieving. I also asked questions by the hundreds, which she patiently answered, no matter how silly some of them may have seemed to her, and I remained in awe at her amazing ability to quote words and principles from so many of her friends in high places for my education.

Commencing with our third session, early in September, Winnie shifted her training program into high gear. Sitting across from me in the library, she placed a typewritten sheet and a stack of file cards on the coffee table and said, "Luke, last night I prepared an outline of the subjects I hope to cover with you during these two days. By planning each of our sessions carefully, I'll be certain I've covered all the points I want to deal with before you leave me for good. By the way, do you know what day this is?"

"Monday."

"Yes, dear boy, it's Monday," she said, giggling, "and it also happens to be Labor Day back in the States."

"Do I get the day off?"

"No, but I'll let you take me to Claridges for dinner this evening."

She picked up the file cards and waved them at me. "From here on I'm going to make it much easier for you to remember the principles we discuss so that later on in life, when you need to apply them, your actions will be almost instinctive. Now, I'll need your full cooperation on this because we're going to file these thoughts into your subconscious mind where they will remain, waiting for recall, as long as you live. In a way, I'm going to program you."

I raised my hand. "Now you've really lost me. . . ."

She closed her eyes, obviously searching for a simple analogy that I would understand. "Luke, that magnificent Norden bombsight of yours . . ."

"What about it?"

"Well, before you go up to drop bombs, there are several bits of important information you must feed into that delicate machine, am I not correct?"

"Yes. We must set certain dials to the altitude we'll be bombing from, the weight of the bombs we're dropping, the speed our plane will be flying on the bomb run. . . ."

"Exactly, and all those elements are programmed into the machine before you reach your target, correct?"

"How do you know so much about our top secret sight?"

"Do you have any idea how many bombardiers have been my guests here during the past few years?"

She selected the file card on top. "I'm going to hand you this card. Like all these others it contains a quote or two from our friends. First, I want you to concentrate on the words and read them to yourself. Then, read them aloud. Finally, I want you to copy the words into your notebook. Then we'll discuss them and you can make any notes you wish before we go on to the next card. We'll program you just as you program your bombsight so that in the future your actions will be as automatic as those of the Norden when a particular situation confronts you. Now do you understand?"

I nodded.

There were two quotations on the first card.

> *Nothing external to me can have any power over me. Walt Whitman.*
> *I shall allow no man to belittle my soul by making me hate him. Booker T. Washington.*

After I had read them aloud, I did as she instructed and copied the words in block letters at the top of a blank page in my notebook. Winnie leaned toward me impatiently, until I finally looked up.

"Luke, we are extremely fragile animals. We can awake with a song on our lips, filled with joyful anticipation of the hours ahead, and then allow a spilled cup of coffee or a flat tire or a harsh word from someone ruin our entire day. Also, we live in a world where envy and hate, unfortunately, seem to be the only activities some people are capable of and those who are so infected, usually because they have already failed at this game of life, will do everything in their power to drag you down to their level on any given day. Ignore them. They can never rain on your parade unless you give them permission to do so. And so it is with events which often produce misfortune and grief in the most perfect of lives. Will you cave in and start sucking your thumb in self-sympathy at every crisis? Or will you always search for the good, even in the most terrible of adversities, reminding yourself that what may seem to be a calamity today may well turn out to be just a detour that will lead you to more success and happiness than you would have ever achieved had you remained on your original path? Remember, nothing external, man or event, has any power over you, *unless you allow it*, because you control your thoughts! Questions?"

I shook my head and she handed me the next card.

> *Every noble work is at first impossible. Thomas Carlyle.*
>
> *When you get into a tight place and everything goes against you, till it seems as though you could not hold on a minute longer, never give up then, for that is just the place and time that the tide will turn. Harriet Beecher Stowe.*

"History is filled, Luke, with stories of those who gave up just when victory was within their grasp. I know you have read Napoleon Hill's *Think and Grow*

Rich, but do you recall his story of Darby's uncle? This old man had just made one of the richest gold strikes ever, and needing expensive machinery to mine it properly, he went back to his relatives and borrowed the money. After the first few cars of ore were shipped off to the smelters, he was positive that soon he would be one of the wealthiest men in the world. Then, tragedy. The vein of gold faded away. Darby's uncle continued to drill and drill until finally he quit, heartbroken, and sold all his equipment to a junkman. Now, the junkman, since he had purchased the equipment so cheaply, decided to gamble a few of his dollars and called in a mining engineer who poked around for several weeks before telling his client that Darby had failed because he knew nothing about 'fault lines' and his figures and tests showed that the vein was still there, *just three feet* from where Darby had stopped digging! Millions of dollars of gold ore were eventually removed from the mine that Darby had abandoned."

She stood and began pacing the floor. "Are you familiar with the term 'second wind'?"

"Yes, the Massachusetts town I lived in, Framingham, is on the route of the famous Boston marathon, which is run every April. It's about nine miles from the start of the race, and at just about the point where the better runners get their second wind while the inexperienced begin dropping out from the pain and exhaustion. I can remember reading the interviews with the winners and they always mentioned the agony they suffered until they got their second wind."

"William James, the psychologist, in one of his essays, Luke, reminded us that second wind is a reality that we can all use to our advantage. It hides, according to him, behind our first effective layer of fatigue, and that fatigue is nature's signal to us that we should stop whatever we are doing before we harm our body. Usually when we hit that obstacle we do stop. No one enjoys pain. However, if an unusual necessity forces us to press onward, a surprising thing happens. The fatigue and pain increase for a while, and then they suddenly vanish and we are fresher than ever. All of us have this mysterious reservoir of energy hidden behind our fatigue obstacle, and if we have the courage to endure the pain and persevere until this energy is released, we can accomplish miracles. Calling on your second wind, Luke, doesn't apply only to athletics. No matter what kind of a difficult task you're engaged in, if you hang on long enough, you'll eventually release an abundant supply of new strength and courage. The important thing is remembering that you do have this marvelous deposit of power that you can call on when you need it most, and knowing this, you'll never quit. Winston Churchill, a few years ago, gave the shortest commencement address in history at one of our posher boys' schools. After a long and tedious introduction, Sir Winston walked slowly to the lectern and said just six words, 'Never, never, never, never give up!' No one has ever said it better."

We did celebrate Labor Day over a late dinner at Claridges after a few whispered words between Winnie and the ancient maître d' somehow reduced our announced waiting time for a table from an hour to less than ten minutes. When the check arrived, following a sinful six-course dinner featuring real tenderloin steak, Winnie insisted on paying despite my protests.

"Luke," she said, placing her fingers over my lips to

silence me, "do you have any idea how long it has been since I've even thought about Labor Day? The last one I can remember celebrating was with my daddy, at Briggs Stadium, stuffing myself with hot dogs and root beer while the Tigers and the Red Sox played a double-header. If being with you can revive those kind of lovely memories in an old woman, the very least she can do is feed you."

Early the next morning we were back in the library, and except for a luncheon break, when Martha brought us sandwiches and tea, the seminar continued through the day. During that long and arduous session, punctuated by two buzz-bomb alerts that we ignored, Winnie covered a wide range of subjects. With the help of her file cards we continued with the learning routine of yesterday, and her friends ranged from Arthur Brisbane teaching me how to utilize my odd moments, "time management," long before anyone had coined such a phrase, to Demosthenes and his gentle warning on avoiding the pitfalls of self-deception.

Winnie's voice had grown hoarse by the time she handed me the last file card from her stack late in the afternoon. "We've accomplished much, Luke, in these past two days, and I pray that you will be able to get to London at least once more. That should be sufficient. Now . . . this last card contains the words of an old Persian philosopher. They may help you, someday, to keep your world in proper perspective when everyone is heaping praise and honors on you for your many accomplishments.

Can you walk on water? You have done no better than a straw. Can you soar in the air?

You have done no better than a fly. Conquer your heart; then you may become somebody. Ansari of Herat.

Those haunting words, in three-dimensional wooden letters, are affixed to a thin sheet of polished white marble that hangs above my office door at our conglomerate's headquarters in Scottsdale. To the few who are bold enough to inquire about their origin, I always reply that they are merely some good advice from an old friend.

XIV

*T*he chilly air in our Nissen hut was filled with smoke, loud conversation, cowboy yells, whistles, and song. All sixteen occupants had flown on the day's mission, a rare happening, and everyone's mood was one of jubilation since we had creamed the railroad yards at Karlsruhe and suffered no losses.

I was sitting up in bed writing to Priscilla, oblivious of the raucous noise and behavior around me, when it suddenly grew very still except for the calm, clipped-accent voice of a BBC newsman coming from Hank's radio.

". . . and it is feared that London may again be in for difficult times. To repeat, our information is still rather sketchy, but the Ministry of Information has confirmed that a tremendous explosion on the west side of London early today was apparently the result of some sort of rocket bomb launched by the Germans from an unknown location in either Belgium or Holland. Our latest estimates indicate that at least thirty are dead, more than two hundred have been hospitalized, and nearly an entire block has been destroyed."

The somber voice continued. "This may be the rumored ultimate secret weapon that Hitler's scientists are believed to have been perfecting at their experimental station, Peenemunde, on an island in the Baltic Sea that has been under Allied surveillance and several bomber attacks since July. If so, it is estimated that this huge missile, the V-2, is capable of delivering more than twelve tons of explosives, and since it travels faster than the speed of sound, unlike the buzz bombs, there is no time to run for cover, since the screeching sound it makes on its approach is never heard until after impact. Also, because of its great speed, it is extremely difficult to detect the approaching rocket on radar in time to sound any sort of warning to the general public. . . ."

I was already dressed, out the door, and riding my bike as swiftly as I could, in the dark, to the officers' club. One of the four phone booths was empty, and twenty agonizing minutes passed before I heard her voice.

"Winnie, are you okay?"

"Yes, of course. Luke? Luke, is that you?"

"It's me."

"What's wrong, dear?"

"Nothing. Just heard the news about that damn V-2 and wanted to make sure you were all right."

"I'm fine. They sent over a second firecracker about thirty minutes ago. We could hear the explosion, but I understand it landed in a meadow in Chelsea, thank God."

"Winnie, isn't there someplace where you can go, outside the city, until we catch up with these rocket boys and put them out of business?"

"I suppose there is, but I'm not leaving Matthew's Court. Who would take care of all my boys?"

I couldn't help laughing. "Listen, lady, if those missiles keep coming, I'm afraid you're going to have plenty of empty rooms. The guys will start heading for Norwich or Cambridge for their fun and games. They get enough thrills when they're flying without having a twelve-ton bomb upsetting their gin and sodas."

"Young man, I do believe you are actually concerned about me."

"You bet I am."

"Good! Now you have some idea how I have felt ever since our first meeting. Each morning when I awake I think to myself, 'Is Luke flying today? If he is, please God, hold him tightly in your hand.' And in the afternoon I'm wondering if you have returned and are safe. You don't know how many times I've fought the urge to ask you to ring me each evening just so I would know you're unharmed and not have to spend half the night tossing and turning. But I just couldn't bring myself to do it. You have enough on your mind without the added burden of having to check in with me every day.

"So you're going to stay in London?"

"I'll be right here, as always."

"Okay, then from now on I will phone you every night so that we can *both* sleep. And I'll see you in three weeks or so."

"You're still coming here?"

"If you can take it, so can I. And didn't you tell me

that we needed at least one more visit to complete our seminar?"

"One should do it."

"I'll be there, rocket bombs or not. Just do me one favor, hon."

"Anything you ask, Luke."

"When you hang up, please sign your name in 'The Hand of God' with the rest of your boys. Promise?"

"I promise . . . and I love you."

During the gray and soggy autumn days of 1944, while Allied ground forces were paying a terrible price in their drive to push the enemy back to the Rhine, our crew added fifteen more pins to Hank Mucci's map in such places as Hannover, Ulm, Koblenz, Osnabrück, and Cologne. Flags had flown at half-mast over every Second Division bomb group headquarters on September 28 after the 445th group, just up the road from us at Tibenham, wandered off course on a mission to Kassel on the previous day and was decimated by more than a hundred enemy fighters. Only seven planes returned out of thirty-seven!

On more than one morning, during our group assembly over England, we would catch fleeting glimpses of long, thin trails of vapor glowing scarlet against the rising sun, streaking high into the heavens above Northern Europe, and we knew that another V-2 was on the way to helpless London. I don't know how many times I caught myself foolishly muttering half aloud, "Duck, Winnie!"

The leave that we had planned on in November was canceled. Replacement crews had hit some sort of bottleneck back in the States, and so Winnie and I didn't complete our seminar of success until early in December, after I had twenty-nine missions under my belt and only six more to go. Three times during our final afternoon session we were interrupted by thunderous explosions, and the last rocket hit so close that the chandelier above our heads swayed menacingly for several minutes.

We celebrated my "graduation" in the evening by returning to Claridges for dinner and later, with the library's fireplace crackling, Winnie retrieved an old and dusty bottle of sherry from her wine cellar.

"Before we uncork this, Luke, there's one more pleasurable duty I must perform." With no further explanation she dashed out of the library and on the way tapped light switches so that the large room was almost in darkness except for a small green-hooded desk lamp. I sat quietly in the shadows until I heard her cry out, "Are you ready?" from the hall.

"I'm ready . . . I think."

I wasn't ready. Had I been, I wouldn't have broken down and cried when Winnie backed into the room, turned, and proudly walked toward me carrying a silver tray on which sat a tall, white-frosted cake ablaze with candles. She was singing, "Happy birthday to you . . . happy birthday to you. . . ."

After she had placed the tray on the coffee table, she sat next to me, gently stroking my back until I finally got control of myself. Her pale face was aglow from the flickering light of twenty-one candles.

"I realize that the big day is not till Tuesday, Luke, but even though Colonel Allen and I are close friends, I doubt that he would have allowed me to deliver this to your cozy quarters at the base so tonight will have to do." She gripped my right hand and forced a tiny smile. "My frosting may not be all that great. I've rather lost my touch since this is the first birthday cake I've baked in . . . in . . . four years. Now, you've got to blow out the candles and make a wish."

My vision was becoming blurred again. "I'm a little out of practice too. The last time I blew out candles on a birthday cake there were only seven of them."

"Go ahead, old man," she said, gently nudging me with her elbow. "I'll stand by in case you need assistance."

While a thin layer of smoke still hovered over the extinguished candles, she half-whispered, "Did you make a wish?"

"Yes. I wished that I might find a way to repay you for all you have given me—the long hours, your love and patience and encouragement, plus a priceless education. There is just no way to show you how grateful I am."

"Luke, you're not supposed to reveal your wish, but if you're concerned about repaying me, that's easy."

"Tell me how, please."

"Just take those seeds that I have planted in your mind, nurture them, keep them free of weeds, and cultivate them until they produce a great harvest that you can share with the world. And never be ashamed to dream big dreams because as you dream, you shall become. Remember our long discussion about our friend, James Allen's little book, *As a Man Thinketh*. All of mankind's great achievements were at first a dream. The oak sleeps in the acorn, the bird waits in the egg, and dreams are the seeds that produce the richest and sweetest fruits. How do you repay me? Just take the talents that God gave you . . . and *use* them!"

She reached under the coffee table and placed a thin

package in my lap, wrapped in gold foil. "Speaking of giving, what's a birthday party without a gift? Happy twenty-one, son."

Before I could remove the glistening paper she said, "Don't open it now, Luke. It's been in my safe for quite some time and it will keep a little longer. Promise you won't unwrap it until you have ended your tour and left England behind and when you do, just follow the instructions."

In the morning before leaving I placed my suitcase near the door in the lower hall and found Winnie at the rolltop desk in the sitting room. "See you after my last mission," I said, waving my cap.

She rose and came toward me slowly. "That would be lovely, Luke, but we mustn't plan on it. As you well know, very often the crews are shipped home as soon as they complete their tour in order to make room for replacements. If that should happen, all I ask is that you write to me often and let me know what is happening in your life."

I opened my arms and she walked into them. "I promise, and in the meantime I'll keep phoning you every night from the base, okay?"

She straightened my tie and nodded. "I'm afraid I'm going to miss you until it hurts."

I cupped her cheeks in my hands and kissed that tiny nose. "I'll never forget you, lady."

XV

Since our skipper, Bob Lally, drank nothing stronger than milk, he rarely accompanied us on our trips to the officers' club. We had stopped inviting him along after the first month or so we were together, although our respect for him as a man and pilot had grown with each mission and we would have flown with him into the jaws of hell.

Hank and Tim and I were sitting at our favorite table, near the jukebox, each trying to guess how long it would take to complete our final six missions. Hank pointed his perpetually unlit cigar at the ceiling. "Listen to that damn downpour. The weather boys tell me that if it doesn't rain every day in December, it snows. I don't think we should count on finishing before the middle of January. If we fly one a week, we'll be lucky. My God," he exclaimed, staring over my shoulder, "look who's here! Will wonders never cease?"

Bob Lally was unbuttoning his dripping trench coat

as he approached our table. He tossed it onto an empty chair, followed by his cap, and slumped down next to me, pointing to my half-empty glass. "Is that beer or ale, Luke?"

"Ale."

"Good," he said, sighing, lifting my glass and draining it. "Now, can I buy you guys a round?"

Tim was the first to recover. "What's wrong, big guy?"

Bob lowered his voice so that we all had to lean forward to hear him over the swinging jukebox. "What I'm going to tell you is absolutely confidential. Is that understood?" He glanced around the table until he had a confirming nod from each of us.

"I've just come from a meeting with Colonel Allen and a Major Anderson from division intelligence. As of noon today, our crew has been taken off combat status."

We all reacted angrily. "Why? What the hell for? What did we do?"

Bob raised both hands. "Hold it, hold it! Now, you all listen very carefully. Colonel Allen told me that everyone on this crew should be very proud of the job they've done. He said that if he had forty crews like ours, being group commander would be a breeze and we would have been promoted to lead crew long ago, except that there were just too many crews ahead of us with seniority. Also, he amazed me by how much he knew about each of us, what our records were in flight school, and Luke, he even knows your bombing average at Carlsbad."

"If we're so great, Bob, how come we're off combat

status?" Tim asked. "It's too late to train us to be a lead crew now. We've got only six to go."

"Wrong," Bob replied, smiling. "We've got only one to go! Thanks to Colonel Allen's recommendation, our crew has been selected by division headquarters to fly just one very special mission. That's all! When it's completed, our tour will be finished and we can go home, but we'll have to spend the next ten days or so, depending on the weather, training for that mission and proving to the brass that we can handle it."

"What kind of a special mission?"

"They wouldn't tell me. 'All in good time,' Allen said. And the man from division, Anderson, made sure I understood how top secret this was. The four of us are not to discuss this with anyone, not even our own crew. If any of the guys ask what kind of practice missions we're flying during the next couple of weeks, we are to say only that we're testing some new bombing tactics for headquarters. Period!"

Hank lit his frayed cigar. "Special mission, huh? Sounds like a real nail-biter, skipper. They're not just going to wipe out our last six in exchange for some little milk run. I smell trouble, big trouble."

Bob shrugged his shoulders. "That's all they told me, and I didn't press it. I did gather, however, that a lot depends on Luke. Most of our practice flights will be to help him get reacquainted with the bombsight, and if this rain stops, we'll begin in the morning."

"That just makes it all the more mysterious," said Tim. "We've got at least a dozen great bombardiers on this base who have led our squadrons, our group, and even the wing on some very tough missions. All experienced. No offense, Luke, but if this secret mission is so important, why aren't they using one of them instead of someone who has never handled the bombsight in combat?"

"There must be a special reason," Bob said, reaching for his wallet, "and we'll know soon enough. Now, can I buy those drinks?"

Thanks to a break in the weather, we managed to fly five practice bombing missions during the following eleven days, and since there was no uninhabited desert for us to bomb, we did our work over water. After takeoff we would head north along the shoreline while climbing to exactly 10,000 feet. The coastal town of Scarborough, approximately 130 miles from our base, was designated "initial point," the beginning of our practice bomb runs. At Scarborough we would turn out into the North Sea on a heading of thirty-eight degrees, and as soon as we were on course, Bob would lock the plane's steering apparatus on automatic pilot, transferring the aircraft's directional control to me and my bombsight. Approximately thirty miles out from Scarborough, we would spot a large white wooden raft floating in the choppy water, courtesy of the United States Navy. This was my aiming point, my target, and on every practice mission I made ten runs at it, each beginning at Scarborough and ending when another hundred-pound practice bomb hit the water and exploded. Twice I actually scored direct hits on the rafts and destroyed them.

Major Harlan Thomas, our group bombardier, accompanied me on each flight, observing my moves, coaching, correcting, encouraging, and taking notes. When we landed, following the fifth flight, he patted my back and said, "I'll tell them you're ready, Luke, for whatever it is they want . . . and good luck."

Each evening, as I had promised, I phoned Winnie, and when I finally told her that we had been taken off combat status to do some testing, there must have been something in my voice that she picked up. "I understand, Luke," she said slowly, "and someday you can tell me all about it." V-2's were now terrorizing London at the rate of ten or twelve each day, and her apartment vacancy rate was very high, but she still refused to flee. How would I ever find her, she asked, if she moved out into the country and I managed to get another pass before shipping home? No, she would hold the fort at Matthew's Court, just in case. . . .

On the morning of December 16 we were all shocked by the news that two panzer divisions, under General Von Rundstedt, had launched a major counterattack against our ground forces, broken through our lines, and were driving into Belgium. With a horrendous fog covering the Continent, our Air Force was helpless and we sat by our radios, day by day, listening to the news grow from bad to worse.

Not until just before Christmas did the fog lift enough for the Eighth Air Force to launch its largest single strike of the war against the airfields of Ardennes in order to give some relief to our troops trapped in what was to be known as the Battle of the Bulge. Our group flew double missions on December 24 and 25, using every plane and crew available . . . except us. Frustrated and ashamed, the four of us kept to ourselves, feeling more like lepers than combat veterans.

I phoned Winnie on Christmas evening and wished her a Merry Christmas. Bing Crosby was singing "I'll

Be Home for Christmas" on the jukebox, and I could hear her repeating over and over, "I love you, Luke." I didn't sleep very well that night.

Five days later, long after everyone else from our hut had gone off to fly another ground support mission, we four were summoned to Colonel Allen's office. With him was Major Anderson from division. While we were all shaking hands, the colonel offered us cigars from a large wooden humidor before asking us to be seated. He pointed toward Major Anderson, who immediately reached into an open briefcase, removed four large glossy photographs, and handed one to each of us.

"Gentlemen," he began in a raspy voice, "I know you are all experienced enough, after twenty-nine missions, so that you can identify what you are looking at as a low-level aerial photograph of an electric generating plant. This particular one has steam turbines and is powered by coal. Note the tall smokestacks and the nearby huge piles of coal under a blanket of snow. The kilowatt capacity of this plant, according to our intelligence reports, is sufficient to handle all the electrical needs of a city of fifty thousand people; however, it is presently being used to provide power almost exclusively for three nearby munitions plants vital to Germany's war effort, and it must be destroyed. That is your target."

Hank Mucci was the first to speak. Waving the photograph, he said, "Forgive me, sir, but if this target is so important, why are you sending only one plane? Isn't this a job for an entire group, at least?"

Anderson nodded. "You're absolutely correct, Lieutenant, and I wish we could do it that way, but we can't. Dropping bombs on this particular target will have to look like an accident. It's going to be up to you men to make it appear as if you wandered off course, away from your group, and mistakenly jettisoned your bombs on this particular chunk of real estate."

"Why?"

"Because this power plant happens to be in Switzerland, three miles inside the border and just northeast of the small Swiss village of Schleitheim. Our State Department, through our embassy in Zurich, has issued several formal complaints in the past four months concerning this blatant violation of neutrality, but they have all been ignored. We have no other choice. The bombs and bullets being manufactured with the help of this 'made in Switzerland' electricity are killing our men every day. It will be up to your crew, alone, to turn off the power and I repeat, for obvious reasons, it must appear to be accidental."

Bob was squirming in his chair, looking very uncomfortable. "Sir, the munitions factories that this power plant is feeding . . . they're in Germany?"

"Yes, all quite close to the border."

"Have we tried to hit them?"

"Several times, with little luck. All three are underground. According to our intelligence, they're working around the clock, and one is the major producer of those nice fat shells that keep knocking you guys out of the sky."

"But bombing Switzerland . . ."

Major Anderson turned toward the colonel and said, "Lieutenant Lally, if you have any problems dealing with this for any reason, you are free to remove yourself from this assignment and we'll understand. That goes for you others too. Just tell us now if you want out."

Bob sighed, rolling his cap over and over in his hands. He turned to face us. "Let's take a vote. Raise your right hand, guys, if you're willing to tackle this one."

Hank quickly spoke up. "Question, sir," he said, looking at Anderson.

"Shoot."

"Does intelligence have any idea how many lives we can save if we do the job right?"

"Lieutenant, they estimate that these three factories are producing about twenty percent of the heavy stuff that Germany is currently using. Putting them out of business will certainly shorten the war and probably save several thousand Allied lives."

We all raised our right hands immediately.

Colonel Allen rose, stepped around his desk, and placed a hand on Bob's shoulder. "Gentlemen, I'm sure you fully realize what an extremely sensitive matter this is to our government, and I'm confident you will not disappoint us. If the weather stays good, we'll go tomorrow. The major will review your detailed flight plan now, with specific times, but briefly, you will take off with the rest of the group as if you were just another plane among thirty-six on our mission to hit the marshaling yards at Freiburg."

He lit his cigar before continuing. "Freiburg is located in that southwestern tip of Germany between France and Switzerland. Your target, the Swiss plant, is approximately thirty-five miles to the southeast. Before our group reaches Colmar and begins its bomb run to Freiburg, you will notify your group leader that you are unable to maintain altitude because of oxygen problems and are dropping out of formation. You will reduce your airspeed so that the group leaves you behind and then you will descend to exactly ten thousand feet before you also turn over Colmar and begin your bomb run on the generating plant. Since we expect no anti-aircraft in that area, your low altitude should present no danger, plus it will make it much easier for Lieutenant Gardiner to score a bull's-eye. After you have dropped your bombs, you will make your way back across southern France, alone. This will be the most dangerous part of your mission since you will have no fighter protection. When you return to England, you will not land here, but at the nearby base, Tibenham, where all ten crew members will be immediately transferred to another plane. You will all wait in that plane until your clothing and personal items are brought to you, and then you will be flown back to the States, where you will be separated from the Army Air Force with your country's eternal gratitude."

He paused and looked at each of us. No one spoke. "Our State Department will immediately tender an official apology to the Swiss for this most unfortunate releasing of explosives over their territory. Your names, of course, will be withheld from the press. Rumors may fly around the base for a while, but we shall do everything in our power to squelch them . . . and fast."

"Let me be sure I understand, sir," I said. "When we are awakened for the usual briefing along with the other crews in the morning, we are to leave all our personal belongings in our hut as we do on every other mission?"

"Correct. As soon as the group returns to our base

following the mission, your crew will be listed as 'missing in action' and your personal things will all be picked up and bagged, following our usual procedure. We'll then fly them to Tibenham, and as soon as you have them you'll be on your way back to the States. That also goes for your enlisted men, although you are not to say a word to them before or after the mission regarding your special assignment. Even though they'll never understand the reason, I'm sure that none of them will complain about completing their tour of duty ahead of schedule."

"Colonel Allen," I said, groping for the right words. "I'm honored that you're letting me do the bombing and I understand that using me and our crew will certainly make the bomb drop look accidental, especially from that low altitude. But what if I should miss the target? What if I fail?"

"You won't fail, Luke," he said, moving over so that both his hands were on my shoulders. "A mutual friend of ours in London, whom I trust implicitly, has assured me that you will never fail at anything that is truly important to you. She said it had something to do with some special friends of yours . . . friends in high places, I believe she said."

Bob and Hank and Tim all turned to stare at me, looking bewildered and puzzled. What could I say?

I just closed my eyes and nodded.

XVI

*D*usk had settled over the base by the time we emerged from Colonel Allen's office. Major Anderson's flight plan review had seemed to take forever, since he had to be certain that we had all important details of our flight, such as checkpoint times and course headings, committed to memory. In the event we crashed, there were to be no records or notes of any sort on board indicating that our plane had been purposely diverted from the group's regular mission in order to bomb a power plant in Switzerland. We even rehearsed special code phrases that the four of us were to use on our intercom so that the other members of our crew would suspect nothing when we dropped out of formation because of "oxygen problems" and eventually "dumped" our bombs in order to lighten our load so that we would have enough fuel to make it back to England.

"Well, gentlemen," said the major after following us

outside, "I'm very confident, now, that this special delivery is in good hands."

Bob invited him to join us at the club for a farewell drink. "Sorry, I've still got a pile of work ahead of me tonight, but you guys had better hurry if you want one for the road. That Freiburg trip tomorrow will be a maximum effort for this group, so they'll be closing the club in less than an hour."

As I turned to leave, the major grasped my hand. "We're counting on you, Luke."

"I'll do my best, sir."

Our table was unusually quiet until Bob raised his mug of ale and said, "It was a great experience to have flown with you guys, and I salute each of you. When I'm an old and retired schoolteacher rocking on my porch, these months we've spent together will be very precious in my book of memories. And just think, we're finally getting our wish. Tim and I will take that Liberator to our own target tomorrow, Hank will guide us to it and bring us home, and Luke will get to show us what a great lead bombardier he would have made. Someone finally recognized the good job we've been doing, mission after mission."

I couldn't resist. "Longfellow," I said, "once wrote that if you only knock long enough and loud enough at the gate, you are sure to wake up somebody."

"There he goes again," Tim groaned.

We had all drained our mugs and were preparing to leave when Hank said, "Hey, buddies, do you realize that this is the last time we'll ever be in this noisy home away from home. What say we bid farewell to this special place with a little class, huh? Will all three of you kindly stand and raise your beer mugs?"

As soon as we were on our feet, Hank turned and heaved his heavy stein into the blazing fireplace and we all did the same. A ten-pound note hastily calmed the irate sergeant on duty who charged at us from behind the bar.

After the others had gone, I phoned Winnie. Waiting for the local operator to connect me with London, I tried to plan exactly what I would say to her, but when I finally heard her voice I began babbling about the weather and God knows what else for several minutes before she interrupted me.

"Luke, stop trying to coddle me. It sounds as if you're trying very hard to find a way to tell me that you will not be returning to London. Am I correct?"

"How did you know?"

"I ran into Colonel Allen last week in Harrods. We had a drink together for old time's sake and we talked about you."

"He didn't tell you what we . . ."

"He told me little or nothing except that you and your crew were being considered for a very special top-secret assignment. That's all. I merely assured him that if he selected you, the possibility of the mission succeeding would be greatly increased, since I didn't think that the word *failure* was in your vocabulary and I told him why. I hope you approve."

"I just wish I had your confidence and faith, Winnie."

"You'll do fine. Just look on this special challenge, whatever it is, as the first leg of your mission in life. Give it all you've got so that the confidence you generate, when you succeed, will fuel you on to your next step . . . and the next . . . and the next."

"I'll do my best, promise you."

"Will you be phoning me after this situation has been . . . handled?"

"I'm sorry, hon, but as it's set up, that will be impossible. There will be no way to contact you when it's over, but I'll write as soon as I'm back in the States."

"I was afraid of that. Do you suppose I'll get any kind of a clue as to this special mischief you're involved in if I pore through *The Times* for the next few days?"

"Knowing you, I'm sure you will. Now, will you please move out into the country until the V-2's stop?"

"I shall take temporary leave from Matthew's Court within the week. Please, dear, write often. The mail will be forwarded, you know."

"I promise."

"Luke, I don't suppose you know what day tomorrow is?"

"Tell me."

"It's the last day of the year, a very special year because God brought you into my life. And tomorrow night is New Year's Eve . . . auld lang syne and all that. . . ."

I knew she was crying, and I felt so helpless.

"Happy New Year, precious man, and know that my love goes with you as long as you live . . . as long as your mission lasts."

Sleep for me was impossible. I realized full well how much the success of our flight depended on me. Everyone in our hut, as I had expected, was awakened for the Freiburg mission, and the early morning temperature was just above freezing when I raced to the latrine, wide awake, to shower and shave. I was dressed before any of the others, and sitting on my cot, waiting for

Bob and Hank and Tim, when I suddenly remembered
Winnie's mysterious birthday present that I wasn't to
open until I had completed my tour and departed from
England. Despite Major Anderson's strict orders to
leave all personal belongings behind, I unlocked my
trunk, removed the foil-covered present, unbuttoned
my shirt, placed the thin package against my chest, and
buttoned up. No one saw me.

At our group's briefing we four tried to act as
surprised and concerned as all the others when Freiburg
was announced as our target. After checking with my
gunners upon arriving at our assigned plane, I joined
Hank in the bomber's nose while Bob and Tim went
through their pilot's check-off list. I couldn't hear what
Hank was saying above the roar of the engines, but he
was smiling and giving me the victory salute while
pointing to the covered bombsight. I spent the next
fifteen minutes programming the memorized data I
had received from Major Anderson into the Norden
and checking all electrical switches before nervously
replacing the instrument's canvas jacket. I could feel
the beating of my heart against Winnie's package.

Since it was much too dangerous for anyone to remain in the nose during takeoffs, Hank and I finally
wriggled through the connecting crawl space to our
usual braced positions for lift-offs, behind Bob and
Tim. Surprisingly our plane's ground crew chief was
still aboard, waiting, as it turned out, for me.

"Lieutenant Gardiner?"

"Yes?"

"Colonel Allen wanted me to be sure you saw what
they painted on the nose of this big bird last night. He
said it was for you."

"For me? You've got to be kidding."

"No, sir. You probably didn't even notice it in the dark. We've still got a few minutes. Follow me."

He preceded me down through the lower hatch, shining his flashlight on the concrete hardstand until I slid through. All preparations on the field had now been completed, and thirty-six pilots awaited the signal flare from the tower to "start engines."

The flashlight's beam rode up the side of the plane's silver fuselage and angled toward the nose, usually the position where flight crews painted pictures of half-naked women or trick names for their favorite plane like "Tahellenbak."

"Do you see it, Lieutenant?"

I saw it—a dark-blue outline of an open hand and in the palm had been painted, in old English lettering, FRIENDS IN HIGH PLACES.

The sergeant turned off his flashlight. "Colonel Allen said that you would understand, sir. Good luck."

Our group formed over East Anglia without incident, and approximately an hour after takeoff we assumed our position in line behind the other two groups. More than a hundred bombers were on their way to Freiburg. As arranged, we were the last plane in the last element of the trailing squadron, and after we had crossed the French coast, Bob Lally checked with our tail gunner.

"Hey, George, how does it feel back there?"

"It's very lonely, skipper. We're a sitting duck with no one behind us. I only pray that the bad guys are all flying ground support today, because if they come up here looking for trouble, we're going to be the first plane in their gunsights."

We remained in formation with all the others until we had climbed to our scheduled bombing altitude of 24,000 feet before the four of us went into our act for the benefit of the other crew members. Bob came on the intercom again, calling the engineer, Bill Lander.

"Bill, Tim and I are having trouble with our oxygen. We've both got our regulators wide open, but we're still not getting very much. Will you check the shut-off valves and the manifold?"

"Will do, Bob."

Twenty minutes passed before we heard Bill's voice again. "All valves and manifold checked, skipper. No problems. Also the supply line. Everything seems okay."

"Luke and Hank, in the nose. Any trouble?"

"Same as you, Bob," Hank reported. "My regulator is wide open, but I don't think I'm getting any oxygen. I'm also starting to get a little dizzy."

"Well, I'm afraid we've had it, guys. We're going to drop out of this little party and get ourselves back down to ten thousand feet before we all start seeing pink elephants. I'll notify group leader. Everybody stay alert, now, because it's going to get mighty lonely up here."

I checked my watch as we began our descent. We were still six minutes from the French city of Colmar, the initial point over which all three groups would turn on their bomb run to Freiburg. More important, as far as I was concerned, Colmar was also the initial point for my bomb run. Since Bob had decreased our ship's airspeed as per our instructions, the three groups gradually pulled away from us and I waited, still in the nose turret, until I could see the squadrons each beginning their wide turn over Colmar. Then, with Hank's help,

I inched backward out of the turret just as we reached the outskirts of the old city.

"Colmar is now directly below us, skipper," I said as calmly as I could. That was my signal to Bob to begin his turn to the right, not toward Freiburg, but several degrees more to the south, on a course heading that would bring us close to the insidious power plant east of Schleitheim. My prearranged announcement also let him know that I was out of the nose turret and prepared to begin our bomb run. I removed the bombsight's cover and turned on all switches. We were approximately eleven minutes from target.

Now it was Bob's turn again. "Luke, we're going to have to get rid of our bombs. There's no way we can get home on the fuel we've got if we lug that load very far. Open your bomb-bay doors and prepare to salvo them."

That told me that he was putting the bomber on automatic pilot and turning the plane's directional control over to me, through my bombsight. I engaged the small clutch lever on the Norden, tugged at the bomb-bay handle, and replied, "Bomb-bay doors are open."

Now I was squatting as low as I could, trying to catch sight of my target ahead. With no assistance. Lead crews always carried an additional officer in the nose turret to help locate the target for their bombardier, but I had no such luxury. I had to find it myself. Also, the bomb-release mechanisms on our planes were usually timed so that the bombs released in train, with one dropping in front of another along a line, on the ground, extending for a quarter of a mile or more. With twelve planes in formation dropping at the same time, the exploding bombs would cut a wide and long swath of devastation, greatly increasing the chances of destroying any target. I couldn't do that. My bombs had to be released all at once so that it would look as if we had jettisoned our load in order to save the plane. I had no margin for error. The bombs would all land in a small cluster, and my aim had to be near perfect.

Major Anderson's aiming instructions to me had been as specific as one could ask. Three miles beyond the village, he said, I would see a large stand of pine trees that would appear, from the air, to be shaped like a huge number seven. The power plant was located exactly where the two lines in the dark-green numeral of firs met. My watch told me we were only four minutes from drop point. I stared ahead, through the Plexiglas. There were pine trees everywhere! Below I could see two small villages. The one on the left had to be Schleitheim, but where was that damn pine grove that looked like a number seven?

"Freiburg is catching hell to our left," one of our waist gunners yelled over the intercom. "There's smoke everywhere!"

I could feel something hard and uncomfortable pressing against my chest when I leaned forward to wipe the plane's small forward window with my hand. Winnie's birthday gift! "Help me, Winnie," I muttered to myself as I stretched over the bombsight in order to get a better view.

Suddenly there it was—slightly to my left! A perfect dark-green seven! I placed my forehead against the Norden's rubber eyepiece and set the vertical crosshair right where the long and short stretch of pines met. Then I began to delicately adjust the vertical dial as we moved closer. Soon I could see the tall chimneys belching dark smoke. I made several more corrections until my target remained exactly at the center of the two thin lines, and held my breath until I finally heard that blessed click. I hastily disengaged the bombsight lever and pressed my intercom button. "I've dumped the bombs, Bob. Now we can go home."

"Roger!"

The plane immediately banked steeply to the right as I was closing the bomb-bay doors. Then it turned to the left in a wide sweeping arc until I heard Bob excitedly exclaim, with words we certainly had not rehearsed, "You're a good man, Luke Gardiner. The power switch has definitely been turned off!"

XVII

*O*ur enlisted men were already engaged in a serious poker game toward the rear of the plane when our C-47 transport lifted off the runway from Scotland's Prestwick Airport early on the first day of the new year.

Following our successful bomb strike, we had managed to escape back across southern France without encountering a single enemy aircraft. After landing at the Tibenham base as instructed, we had waited for more than two hours before our personal effects were brought to us from Marley. We were still in our combat clothes when we were flown to the American base at Prestwick, where all ten of us were fed in a small dining room before we were driven to our quarters and told to wait for further orders. They were delivered in a large manila packet later by an elderly captain who smilingly waved as he was leaving and said, "Lucky dogs!"

We were to be flown from Prestwick to Goose Bay, Labrador, and from there to Boston. From Boston we would be driven to nearby Camp Myles Standish, but instead of receiving the usual thirty-day rehabilitation and recuperation leave before assignment to another base, we would be paid, including railroad fare to our hometown, honorably discharged, and separated immediately from the United States Army Air Force. Although the enlisted men all cheered loudly when they read their orders, none of them raised any touchy questions as to why we were being sent home in such a mysterious manner before completing our tour of duty. I am convinced, to this day, that all of them knew, or at least suspected, the truth.

The interior of our C-47 had obviously been furnished to transport high-ranking brass. Behind the four-man crew there were comfortable leather seats for all of us that, to our amazement, reclined. Most important, the plane was heated, a luxury we had never enjoyed before, and there was a large refrigerator in the rear stocked with soft drinks, cookies, and sandwiches.

Bob had his clipboard out and was writing another letter; Hank was agonizing over a crossword puzzle, and Tim had his face against one of the small windows, scowling at the ocean far below. All four of us were suffering from both a physical and mental letdown, not only from the terrible pressures of the past twenty-four hours, but from all those frightening months of having lived so close to death. We were elated for having survived, and yet it was a joy tinged with guilt, guilt for still being alive while so many wonderful guys we knew were gone forever.

I thought of Winnie and her son, Dana. Such a

terrible waste. Why is he gone while I'm still breathing? What was his treehouse like? Is it still intact and is anybody playing in it these days?

Winnie. I reached down into my small travel bag and removed her gift that I had carried close to my heart on that last mission. I wasn't to open it until I had finished my tour and left England. Now? I carefully peeled the gold foil away from a thin red leather book. On its jacket cover, embossed in gold, were the words THE SEEDS OF SUCCESS. Clipped to the cover was a folded letter, written on blue-lined paper.

December 1, 1944

Dear Luke,

By the time you open this package there will probably be an ocean between us, but neither distance nor time will ever really separate us.

You were a marvelous student and it was such a great thrill to see how enthusiastically you embraced the wisdom of my friends in high places. Save all of your notes. They will be a great source of comfort and strength when things do not seem to be going exactly as you planned. Do not, however, rely on your notes alone. There are many more friends also waiting to assist you in every bookstore and library. The only problem, of course, is that they cannot come to you. You must search them out, and when you do, they will assist you in any situation, no matter how difficult. Never stop reading, Luke. Never!

I have spent countless hours trying to decide what would be an appropriate gift for your birthday. Since I am getting quite close to the end of my life, have no needs and no heirs, I considered a gift of money large enough so that you would be able to adjust to civilian life without the usual pressures that are certain to concern all our young veterans. For one rather silly morning I even thought about giving you my old Jaguar that you like so much, but friends tell me that it will be several years, after this war is over, before you'll be able to get that temperamental beast serviced properly in the States.

Actually the ultimate choice of your gift was quite easy. I came to the conclusion that it had to be related to the long hours we spent together in our success seminar and it had to be something that would constantly remind you of the most important success principles I taught you, principles that would help you attain more money or Jaguars, if those were your goals, than I could ever give you.

And so, I bequeath to you, with all of my love, this tiny old book. An antiquarian in Liverpool sold me the ancient volume with its silky blank pages, and I carefully copied the principles that were most important on the fragile pages before having the jacket embossed in gold with the original title of the book I had set out to write in honor of my father. This was going to be Dana's twenty-first-birthday gift, and I almost burned it when he was killed. I'm glad I didn't.

My message to you regarding The Seeds of Success *is exactly what I would have told Dana had he been spared. More than once you have heard me say that life is a mission that most of us are trying to fly without any flight plan because they never gave us one in school. Life is indeed a mission, but none of us can handle it when we mistakenly try to measure it in years or months or even weeks.*

Luke, every day is our life in miniature, and whether we like it or not, we must string each day together, like beads, just one at a time. When you awake, the day ahead is the only one you can deal with. Live it so that you have no regrets when your head hits the pillow at night, and you will have another golden bead for your string. String enough lovely beads together and you will eventually have the priceless necklace of a good life. There is no other way; there is no other path to success and happiness.

I have asked many favors of you over the months we've been together, and you have never disappointed me. I now ask one more, the most important of all.

Each morning after you have returned to the States, take just a few minutes to read The Seeds of Success. *Do it daily until it becomes as much an early morning habit as shaving or combing your hair. When you do, you will plant seeds of love and sharing and courage and perseverance into your subconscious mind that will*

140

produce a glorious harvest throughout the day because you will have programmed yourself for success, not failure; for joy, not despair; for love, not hate; for giving, not hoarding. And never forget, as you are reading, that the principles are not ours, but only a distillation of what we have learned from so many of our beloved friends, yours and mine.

Later in your life, much later, after you have proved to yourself that using The Seeds of Success *has borne good fruit, you are free to share them with the world, if you wish, providing that you are willing to offer yourself as a living example of their value. When and if you do, just tell them that it was your legacy from an old lady who loved you very much.*

God bless,
Winnie

I folded the letter carefully and tucked it between the pages in the book. Each page seemed to contain only a few lines of her delicate handwriting, but I couldn't bring myself to read any of it. This was not the time. I forced my chair back into a deep reclining position and fell asleep.

We landed at Goose Bay, Labrador, late in the afternoon and were told that our flight to Boston was scheduled for ten the following morning. All of us had dinner at the enlisted men's mess hall, and on the way out, Bob and I were attracted to a large framed parchment hanging in the sparse hallway. It was titled "Song of Thanks," and underneath the text a caption informed us that it had been written by Baron Guenther Von Huenefeld, on April 13, 1928, after he and his crew had successfully completed the world's first east-to-west transatlantic airplane flight, from Dublin to Greenly Island, Labrador. I read the poignant words three times:

> Silent I ponder. Ended is the flight,
> And He whose hands upheld us in the air,
> Whose grace has calmed the snowstorm and the
>   night,
> Is now with me and folds my hands in prayer.

Long after the others were fast asleep I turned on the small gooseneck lamp attached to my bedpost and opened Winnie's book.

Except for two days in 1974, when I was recovering from surgery, there has not been a day in the past forty years when I have faced the world without first reading *The Seeds of Success.*

XVIII

THE SEEDS OF SUCCESS

God, I thank you for this day.

I know I have not accomplished as yet all you expect of me, and if that is your reason for bathing me in the fresh dew of another dawn, I am most grateful.

I am prepared, at last, to make you proud of me.

I will forget yesterday, with all its trials and tribulations, aggravations and setbacks, angers and frustrations. The past is already a dream from which I can neither retrieve a single word nor erase any foolish deeds.

I will resolve, however, that if I have injured anyone yesterday through my thoughtlessness, I will not let this day's sun set before I make amends, and nothing I do today will be of greater importance.

I will not fret the future. My success and happiness does not depend on straining to see what lurks dimly on the horizon but to do, this day, what lies clearly at hand.

I will treasure this day, for it is all I have. I know that its rushing hours cannot be accumulated or stored, like precious grain, for future use.

I will live as all good actors do when they are onstage—only in the moment. I cannot perform at my best today by regretting my previous act's mistakes or worrying about the scene to come.

I will embrace today's difficult tasks, take off my coat, and make dust in the world. I will remember that the busier I am, the less harm I am apt to suffer, the tastier will be my food, the sweeter my sleep, and the better satisfied I will be with my place in the world.

I will free myself today from slavery to the clock and calendar. Although I will plan this day in order to conserve my steps and energy, I will begin to measure my life in deeds, not years; in thoughts, not seasons; in feelings, not figures on a dial.

I will remain aware of how little it takes to make this a happy day. Never will I pursue happiness, because it is not a goal, just a by-product, and there is no happiness in having or in getting, only in giving.

I will run from no danger I might encounter today, because I am certain that nothing will happen to me that I am not equipped to handle with your help. Just as any gem is polished by friction, I am certain to become more valuable through this day's adversities, and if you close one door, you always open another for me.

I will live this day as if it were Christmas. I will be a giver of gifts and deliver to my enemies the gift of forgiveness; my opponents, tolerance; my friends, a smile; my children, a good example, and every gift will be wrapped with unconditional love.

I will waste not even a precious second today in anger or hate or jealousy or selfishness. I know that the seeds I sow I will harvest, because every action, good or bad, is always followed by an equal reaction. I will plant only good seeds this day.

I will treat today as a priceless violin. One may draw harmony from it and another, discord, yet no one will blame the instrument. Life is the same, and if I play it correctly, it will give forth beauty, but if I play it ignorantly, it will produce ugliness.

I will condition myself to look on every problem I encounter today as no more than a pebble in my shoe. I remember the pain, so harsh I could hardly walk, and recall my surprise when I removed my shoe and found only a grain of sand.

I will work convinced that nothing great was ever achieved without enthusiasm. To do anything today that is truly worth doing, I must not stand back shivering and thinking of the cold and danger, but jump in with gusto and scramble through as well as I can.

I will face the world with goals set for this day, but they will be attainable ones, not the vague, impossible variety declared by those who make a career of failure. I realize that you always try me with a little, first, to see what I would do with a lot.

I will never hide my talents. If I am silent, I am forgotten, if I do not advance, I will fall back. If I walk away from any challenge today, my self-esteem will be forever scarred, and if I cease to grow, even a little, I will become smaller. I reject the stationary position because it is always the beginning of the end.

MISSION: SUCCESS!

I will keep a smile on my face and in my heart even when it hurts today. I know that the world is a looking glass and gives back to me the reflection of my own soul. Now I understand the secret of correcting the attitude of others and that is to correct my own.

I will turn away from any temptation today that might cause me to break my word or lose my self-respect. I am positive that the only thing I possess more valuable than my life is my honor.

I will work this day with all my strength, content in the knowledge that life does not consist of wallowing in the past or peering anxiously at the future. It is appalling to contemplate the great number of painful steps by which one arrives at a truth so old, so obvious, and so frequently expressed. Whatever it offers, little or much, my life is now.

I will pause whenever I am feeling sorry for myself today, and remember that this is the only day I have and I must play it to the fullest. What my part may signify in the great whole, I may not recognize, but I am here to play it and now is the time.

I will count this day a separate life.

I will remember that those who have fewest regrets are those who take each moment as it comes for all that it is worth.

This is my day!
These are my seeds.
Thank you, God, for this precious garden of time.

XIX

I showered and shaved and selected a dark pinstripe suit from the bedroom's mammoth closet. Since my usual attire in Scottsdale, even at board meetings, is as casual as possible, buttoning up my vest and putting a respectable knot in the maroon silk tie seemed to take forever.

Voices of the BBC crew filtered in from the sitting room, where they were setting up their lights for my scheduled three-o'clock interview, and occasionally I could hear Sidney offering words of advice. After viewing the rubble on Matthew's Court, I didn't feel like talking to anyone, much less do a television interview, but I just couldn't bring myself to cancel it. Winnie would never have approved.

There had been a pretty steady diet of television appearances during the past five years, ever since Gardiner Industries had passed the billion-dollar annual sales milestone, and I had become quite comfortable before the camera thanks to some great advice I had received from my close friend and neighbor, Rita Davenport, who had her own popular television show on Phoenix's Channel 5. Years ago Rita, with plenty of collusion from Priscilla, finally got me to agree to make my first television appearance on her morning program, and I still recall how nervous I had been when she picked me up and drove me to the studio. I also remember her wise words of advice that I have followed ever since.

"Luke Gardiner," she said, shaking her head, "I'm the one who should be nervous, interviewing someone like you, and that will apply to any program you do anywhere, even in New York. Just relax, don't look at the camera, keep your hands still, and give me that handsome smile. And when I ask you questions, just answer as naturally as you would if we were at a cocktail party. Most important, if you don't know, say so. Just be yourself and you'll be great, believe me."

"Careful of the wires, Mr. Gardiner," Sidney warned as he led me toward a Chesterfield sofa that was bathed in bright orange from three floodlights. Sitting crosslegged on the sofa and repeating numbers into a handheld microphone was a striking brunette who paused when she saw us approaching.

"Miss Warner," Sidney said as he bowed slightly, "this is Luke Gardiner. Luke, Miss Warner will be conducting your interview."

"Welcome to London, Mr. Gardiner. It's an honor to meet you, and we're extremely grateful for this opportunity to chat with you before the big day tomorrow."

I sat next to her and we exchanged small talk for

several minutes while a bearded fellow in blue jeans, carrying a bulky television camera on his right shoulder, changed positions several times until he raised his right thumb to indicate that he was satisfied.

We would tape for approximately nine minutes, I was informed, so I should try to keep my responses as brief as possible, but I wasn't to concern myself about the time. If we ran over, they would edit the tape before showing it on this evening's news. At last the camera was rolling.

After an introduction filled with superlatives regarding my life's accomplishments, and mention of the scheduled groundbreaking tomorrow afternoon in Hampstead Heath, Miss Warner said, "Tell us, Mr. Gardiner, why are you making such a tremendous investment here in England since most of American capital has shunned us for many years? Do you know something that they don't?"

"No, I hardly think so. What I'm doing here is breaking one of the cardinal rules of good corporate financing by investing with my heart instead of my head. But since I have no stockholders to answer to, this is a risk I take willingly and gladly."

Miss Warner's dark brown eyes opened wide, and she leaned forward. "Would you mind explaining?"

"The building I'm erecting in London symbolizes, for me, the fulfillment of a lifetime mission that I was sent on, following the war, by a very special woman who lived here, on Matthew's Court. I'm trying in my own way to repay at least a part of my great debt to her. . . ."

With an encouraging nod now and then from Miss Warner, I related the entire Winnie Marlow story from the evening I first met her through the long sessions of our success seminar, when she introduced me to her friends in high places. I ended by describing her birthday gift to me and how living with the powerful words of *The Seeds of Success* day after day had affected and shaped my life.

I was certain we had exceeded our allotted nine minutes by the time I had finished, but my interviewer was not about to stop. She was obviously experienced enough to sense that she might be onto something special.

"Mr. Gardiner, in all the material I've managed to read about you and your many successes, I can't recall any reference to this mysterious woman of London who obviously had such a great influence on your life."

"That's because I've never talked about her before to any of the media people. It's a very personal and precious part of my past that I've managed to keep very close to my heart, and until now only my wife and two sons knew the story."

She gasped. "Are you telling me that we have an exclusive here?"

I smiled and nodded. "Guess you do."

"Amazing! And this special lady responsible for your success, Winnie Marlow, did she continue to advise you after you began your meteoric rise in the business world?"

It was difficult to mouth the words. "After I returned to the States, she never replied to a single letter of mine. Not one. This morning I discovered why."

The microphone moved closer to my face. I inhaled deeply and said, "Only a day after I completed my tour of duty and left England, her apartment was destroyed by a V-2 rocket."

Miss Warner bit on her lower lip. "I'm so sorry. Then this huge plant you are building is, in a way, your memorial to her?"

I nodded and glanced up to see a mystified Sidney, standing flat-footed next to the cameraman. His mouth was open. Close by was a tall woman holding a legal pad, waving her index finger in a circular motion, signaling Miss Warner to bring the interview to a close.

"One final question, Mr. Gardiner. I must ask this. Whatever happened to your gift, that small book—*The Seeds of Success?*"

"I have it with me because it still helps me to begin every day on a positive note. Tomorrow, when I honor Winnie, I shall make copies of its contents available to all the media present. Hopefully they will agree that its simple but priceless message should be circulated widely."

"Sir," Miss Warner exclaimed, grasping my hand, "if you're an example of what can be achieved by using *The Seeds of Success* every day, I'm sure the whole world will be ready to give it a go. Thank you for your valuable time, and may the sun shine brightly on you tomorrow!"

The BBC crew returned my sitting room to its former pristine state and were gone within fifteen minutes, leaving me alone with Sidney. I walked over to the small wet bar and plunked some ice cubes into two glasses. "Drink, Sidney?"

"Yes, sir, I think I need one."

We drank in silence for several moments before Sidney said, "I wished you had briefed me on all that, sir. We could have gotten some great mileage in the press from such a touching and inspiring story."

I sipped my drink and nodded. "You're probably right, as usual, lad, but you must understand that I had no plans to turn that interview into a tearjerker in order to promote our business image. It all just spilled out. I was going to pay homage to Winnie in tomorrow's speech, distribute copies of *The Seeds of Success* to the press, and dedicate the building to her. Low key. British style. But that was before my trip to Matthew's Court this morning. I guess telling it all to Miss Warner was a good catharsis for me."

"And you do have copies of *The Seeds of Success* to distribute?"

"Yes. Margaret copied its few words from the book with her word processor and ran off fifty sets before I left Scottsdale."

He grinned nervously. "Do you suppose your PR man could have an advance copy?"

"Of course."

I opened my briefcase and handed him three typed sheets of stationery stapled together in their upper left-hand corners. His eyes scanned the pages.

"This is it?" he asked incredulously.

"That's it. You were perhaps expecting two hundred pages of phony pop psychology or another far-out discourse on how to manage one's business on a skateboard?"

"My God! Unbelievable!" He continued muttering to himself while he carefully folded the pages and tucked them into his inside breast pocket. "Well, sir, I'll let you get some rest. It's been quite a day, and the big one is still ahead of us. By the way, they'll be airing your interview at seven this evening, in case you want to watch. Something tells me that we're going to have a larger crowd than we had expected at the groundbreaking tomorrow."

"I'll watch tonight. There's always been a lot of ham in me. See you in the morning, Sidney, and thanks for everything. You're a good man."

"Thank you, sir. Good night, now."

"Sidney."

"Yes, Mr. Gardiner?"

"If I may make one suggestion. Tomorrow morning, while you're having breakfast, read *The Seeds of Success*. It will make a big difference in your day, believe me."

"Oh, I believe you, sir . . . I believe you!"

XX

*J*et lag was beginning to take its toll, and so I took a nap before phoning room service for dinner. Fortunately I remembered to look at my watch just as the food arrived on an elegant brass cart, and when I turned on the television set, Miss Warner was introducing me. My dour waiter finally departed without seeming at all impressed at the sight of a Dorchester guest watching himself on the tube, but I'm pretty certain that Rita Davenport would have been proud of my performance.

Afterward I reviewed the notes for my groundbreaking speech, the next afternoon, before phoning my wife. With the eight-hour time difference between London and Scottsdale, I reached her while she was having lunch. This trip had been one of those rare occasions when I had traveled anywhere without Priscilla, but she was chairperson for a large charity ball at the Arizona Biltmore, only three days away, and we both decided that her prime responsibility was at home riding herd on all the committees involved in making the giant bash a success. After forty-five minutes of chatter, my still frugal lady reminded me of the telephone bill we were running up, wished me luck on the speech, told me she still loved me, and hung up.

The phone rang as soon as I dropped it onto its cradle. "Mr. Gardiner, this is Miss Warner, and I do apologize for disturbing you, but something extremely unusual has just occurred and I thought you should be informed immediately."

"I'm glad you called. Gives me the opportunity to thank you again for the kind way you handled me. I enjoyed the program very much."

"Oh, thank you, sir. I thought it went very well. In any event, our station's switchboard operator rang me up at my flat around fifteen minutes ago with an urgent message for me to telephone a Lord Banbury. I know him and Lady Banbury only by reputation, but they've been quite prominent in society circles hereabouts for many years and have a lovely country manor just southeast of London in Surrey, near the town of Guildford."

"And after seeing us on television tonight they would like a hefty contribution from my company for their favorite charity?"

"Oh, no . . . no, sir, nothing like that," she replied, sounding as if she were having difficulty breathing.

"I'm afraid I don't understand, Miss Warner."

"I do hope you are sitting down, sir."

"I am now," I replied as I lowered myself onto the sofa.

"Mr. Gardiner, I have some extraordinary and wonderful news for you!"

"Tell me."

"Your Winnie Marlow is alive!"

The receiver slipped from my hand, and when I finally retrieved it, I could hear Miss Warner repeating my name over and over.

"Sir, sir, did you hear what I said?"

"I'm not sure. Say it again."

"Winnie Marlow is alive! Lord Banbury didn't know how to locate you after he saw our program this evening, so he contacted the station. Would you like to see her?"

I could hear Miss Warner's voice, but I was having difficulty with her words. Winnie alive? Could it be? Or was this Lord Banbury call from some kind of nut getting his kicks? So many questions were racing through my mind that I didn't know what to ask first. Finally I inhaled and heard myself saying, "Where is she?"

"She's a house guest at the Banbury estate, where she has been living for almost the past forty years. Lord Banbury said that if I managed to contact you, I was to extend his invitation to you to come visit Mrs. Marlow at the manor."

"Did you speak with her?"

"I asked if I could, but he said that would be impossible."

"Impossible? What else did he say?"

"That's about all, sir. He brushed off my other questions and told me he would be happy to furnish you with all the details in person. Quite mysterious, I thought."

"And you're positive you were talking to Banbury?"

"Oh, yes, I've seen and heard him many times on radio and television."

"I must see her."

"Are you free now, sir?"

"Completely."

"If you'd like, I'm not far from the Dorchester, and I'd be glad to come by and drive you to Guildford. Depending on the traffic, it will be only a thirty- or forty-minute drive, and I'll phone Lord Banbury to tell him we're on the way."

"Miss Warner, you are an angel!"

"I'll be there in ten minutes."

"Great. I'll be waiting outside the front entrance. Oh, one more favor, please."

"Yes, sir?"

"No television cameras!"

"I promise."

We spoke very little on the ride to Guildford after Miss Warner apologized because of the side streets she had to take through London in order to avoid theater traffic. As we moved out into the suburbs she said, "I just remembered a rather strange question Lord Banbury asked me."

"What's that?"

"He wondered if your personal appearance had changed very much since the war."

"In forty years? Is he kidding? Oh, I guess my weight is about the same and the eyes are still brown, but the hair is white, of course, and there are plenty of wrinkles in the old face. All earned. I can't believe it. I just can't believe it. Winnie, still alive! What's Banbury's connection with her, did he say?"

"No, but we'll find out soon enough," she replied as we passed through open wrought iron gates and followed a long circular driveway to a well-lit portico. As

I was reaching for a shiny brass door knocker, the massive wooden door swung open and a balding butler bowed and said, "Miss Warner, Mr. Gardiner, please, come in. Lord Banbury is expecting you."

We were led down a long hallway flanked by several life-size marble statues, and shown into a large room that immediately triggered bittersweet memories. Dark wood cabinets and shelves. Books rising in tiers to a glistening mosaic ceiling. The smell of burning wood in the fireplace. A tall figure rose from his seat near the fire and approached us slowly with the help of a cane. His magnificent voice echoed through the room. "Welcome," he said, transferring his cane to his left hand and extending his right, "I'm glad that you both could come."

After the butler poured glasses of sherry for us, he vanished and Lord Banbury commenced by saying, "Mr. Gardiner, it is a great honor to meet you. I was very impressed with your story tonight. Excellent program."

"Well, I'm certainly glad you saw it, sir."

His white hair glistened in the light of the fireplace as he nodded and said softly, "Winnie saw it too. Amazing set of circumstances, really."

"She's here with you?"

"Oh, yes, she's been with us now for almost four decades. Unfortunately she has no idea where she is or who she is. Total amnesia during all the years she has been under our care."

I stared into the fire for several minutes before I could continue the conversation. "Is her condition the result of the explosion that gutted her apartment?"

"We don't know for a certainty, Mr. Gardiner,

although the very best medical people I've had attending her through the years agree that was the probable cause. Actually how she ever survived that damn V-2 is a mystery as well as a miracle. She was found wandering in Hyde Park, wearing only a light dress in almost freezing weather on the afternoon of New Year's Day, 1945. Many survivors of our bombings often lapsed into a form of amnesia, and *The Times* frequently ran photos of these Jane or John Does in an effort to locate their relatives. Of course, Winnie had no relatives, but thank God I saw her picture and had her released in my care and I have done my best to provide her with the tender loving care she certainly deserves. Actually nothing I could possibly do would ever repay my debt to her."

I smiled wanly. "You too?"

His voice cracked. "I suspect that you and I are just two of many, Mr. Gardiner. I owe Winnie everything. Before the war I had a small auto parts business that was facing bankruptcy, and she saved me with a large loan. With her help and encouragement I managed to build the largest organization of its kind in the United Kingdom before retiring."

"That sounds like her, Lord Banbury. From all she told me I gathered that she had a considerable fortune."

"Not quite correct, sir. She was never a wealthy woman. Her philosophy of life was to share everything she possessed with those who needed her help, and although she did earn several million through her shrewd business dealings, she was always giving it away. I learned that she supported at least a dozen charities, and when that bomb hit, she was almost penniless."

"I'll never forget what she shared with me. You said that she did see the program tonight?"

"Ah, yes. However, what I neglected to tell you is that although my doctors claimed there was apparently nothing wrong with her vocal chords, Winnie has uttered not a single word in all the time she has been here, nor has she made any attempt to communicate with us through writing or even hand signals. Completely passive. The psychiatrists believe it is some form of regression caused by the trauma of the explosion."

"Not even a sound from her . . . all these years?"

"Not until tonight. My wife and I were in here enjoying your interview when Winnie's nurse came rushing in to tell us that Winnie was also watching your program in her room and she was sobbing, rocking back and forth in her wheelchair, moaning and pointing frantically at the screen. I ran back to her room, so excited that I forgot my cane, and she was still moaning and pointing at your image . . . the first sounds I had heard from her since she has been under this roof. I was certain that she had recognized you, and that's why I phoned Miss Warner immediately."

I bowed my head, struggling to hold back the tears. "May I see her, sir?"

The old man rose with great effort, hobbled toward me, and placed his large hand on my shoulder. "Of course you may. Come, I'll take you to her room. The nurse is expecting us."

Lord Banbury led me through several rooms and down a hall before pausing at a closed door on which WINNIE was painted in old English letters. He patted my back and I turned the knob, entering a dimly lit room that was richly furnished. When the stocky nurse saw me enter, she stepped away from the figure in the wheelchair, near a satin-covered bed, and nodded in my direction as she passed me. On her way out she turned on the overhead light.

The slight figure in the chair was sitting with her back to me. I turned to my right and almost tiptoed in a wide arc until I had completed a half-circle and was facing her. Then I moved nearer and knelt before the old woman who had transformed my life. Now I was close enough to reach out and touch her small, pale hands resting on the chair wheels.

She was staring down at her lap and I waited, speechless, until she raised her head and I saw those memorable green eyes gradually open wide. I leaned toward her, and she raised both her quivering hands until they were resting on my cheeks. She was smiling!

"Oh, Dana, my Dana, I thought I had lost you forever. Where have you been, child?"

I didn't know what to say. I placed my right cheek, now moist with tears, against Winnie Marlow's forehead and sobbed, "I've been playing. . . ."

"Didn't you hear me calling you, son?"

"I'm sorry, dear. I would have come if I had heard you."

She nodded. "Of course you would. I should have known where to look for you."

"Where, Mother?"

"In the treehouse, of course. Up high, with all your friends . . . in the treehouse."

ABOUT THE AUTHOR

Og Mandino is the most widely read inspirational and self-help author in the world. His 12 books have sold more than 18 million copies in 17 languages. He is also a member of the International Speakers Hall of Fame and one of the most sought-after speakers in the nation. Countless thousands, the world over, have acknowledged, in their letters, the great debt they owe Og Mandino for the miracle his words have wrought in their lives. His beloved masterpieces include *The Greatest Salesman in the World*, *The Greatest Secret in the World*, *The Greatest Success in the World*, *The Greatest Miracle in the World*, *The Christ Commission*, *Og Mandino's University of Success*, *The Choice*, and *Mission: Success!*

Heartwarming Books of
Faith and Inspiration

☐ 26359	JUST LIKE ICE CREAM, Johnson	$2.75
☐ 24452	LIFE AFTER LIFE, Moody	$3.95
☐ 23928	THE SECRET KINGDOM, Robertson & Slosser	$3.50
☐ 25669	THE HIDING PLACE, Boom	$3.95
☐ 25345	THE RICHEST MAN IN BABYLON, Clason	$3.50
☐ 27375	FASCINATING WOMANHOOD, Andelin	$4.50
☐ 27085	MEETING GOD AT EVERY TURN, Marshall	$3.95
☐ 26753	ACT OF MARRIAGE, LeHayes	$4.50
☐ 25551	CONFESSIONS OF A HAPPY CHRISTIAN, Ziglar	$3.50
☐ 25155	A SEVERE MERCY, Vanauken	$3.95
☐ 27144	BIBLE AS HISTORY, Keller	$5.50
☐ 27417	HOW TO WIN OVER DEPRESSION, LeHayes	$4.50
☐ 26249	"WITH GOD ALL THINGS ARE POSSIBLE," Life Study Fellowship	$3.95
☐ 25993	HEALING, MacNutt	$4.50
☐ 27088	MYTHS TO LIVE BY, Campbell	$4.95

Buy them at your local bookstore or use this handy coupon for ordering: